Ancient Warfare: A Very Short Introduction

VERY SHORT INTRODUCTIONS are for anyone wanting a stimulating and accessible way into a new subject. They are written by experts, and have been translated into more than 45 different languages.

The series began in 1995, and now covers a wide variety of topics in every discipline. The VSI library now contains over 500 volumes—a Very Short Introduction to everything from Psychology and Philosophy of Science to American History and Relativity—and continues to grow in every subject area.

Titles in the series include the following:

Harry Sidebottom

ANCIENT WARFARE

A Very Short Introduction

OXFORD
UNIVERSITY PRESS

OXFORD
UNIVERSITY PRESS

Great Clarendon Street, Oxford OX2 6DP

Oxford University Press is a department of the University of Oxford.
It furthers the University's objective of excellence in research, scholarship,
and education by publishing worldwide in

Oxford New York

Auckland Cape Town Dar es Salaam Hong Kong Karachi Kuala Lumpur
Madrid Melbourne Mexico City Nairobi New Delhi Taipei Toronto
Shanghai

With offices in

Argentina Austria Brazil Chile Czech Republic France Greece
Guatemala Hungary Italy Japan South Korea Poland Portugal
Singapore Switzerland Thailand Turkey Ukraine Vietnam

Oxford is a registered trade mark of Oxford University Press
in the UK and in certain other countries

Published in the United States
by Oxford University Press Inc., New York

British Library Cataloguing in Publication Data

Data available

Library of Congress Cataloging in Publication Data

Sidebottom, Harry. Ancient warfare / Harry Sidebottom.
p. cm. — (Very short introduction)
Summary: "This book explores the ways in which ancient society thought about
conflict. Many aspects of ancient warfare are examined from philosophy to the
technical skills needed to fight" — provided by publisher
Includes bibliographical references and index.
1. Military art and science — History —To 500.   2. Military history, Ancient.
3. Civilization, Western.   I. Title.   II. Very short introductions.
U33.S52 2004 355.4'09'01—dc22 2004024151

ISBN 978-0-19-280470-9

15

Contents

Preface

[handwritten: Grk + RME 750 BC → 650 AD]

[handwritten in right margin: → significance of war in CULTURE ↑]

This book deals with war between about 750 BC and AD 650. It
concentrates on the classical cultures of Greece and Rome, although
some of their enemies, peoples such as the Persians, Carthaginians,
Germans, Huns, Arabs, and so on, get a look in. There are reasons
beyond the author's academic specialization for this focus. *[handwritten: enemies]*

War was at the core of the classical cultures. Although, contrary to
popular ideas, they were not always at war, and when they were they
did not always seek open battle. The Greeks and Romans for long
periods of time were generally successful in war, and war was never
far from their minds. The ancient Mediterranean world produced
sophisticated thinking specifically about war, much of which is still of
relevance today. Concepts drawn from war were also used to structure
thinking in many other areas. War was considered to be one of the main
ways to distinguish one culture from another. Within the classical
cultures, war was central to the construction of masculinity and
thoughts about the differences between men and women. At the most
intimate level, ideas from war were used by individuals to understand
and construct their own personalities. In the Greek and Roman worlds
almost everything you read, heard, or looked at could evoke warfare.

The Greeks and Romans liked to believe that they made war in a
way that was different both from earlier peoples and from other
contemporary peoples. This makes for a discrete area of study.

Influence on modern day war

Some modern scholars have picked up on the classical cultures' ideas of their distinctiveness in war-making and, linking this to classical influences on modern Western culture, have come up with the concept of a 'Western Way of War'; a continuity of practices that they claim runs from ancient Greece to the modern West. Exploration and re-evaluation of this concept is central to this book.

Those scholars who see a continuity in a 'Western Way of War' tend to define it as follows. It is the desire for open, decisive battle, which aims at the annihilation of the enemy. Ideally it is conducted by heavily armed infantry fighting hand to hand. The battle is won by courage, which is instilled in part by training and discipline. This is often linked to the combatants having political freedom and being landowners – so-called 'civic-militarism'. This 'Western Way of War' is seen as having been invented by the Greeks, inherited by the Romans, and somehow surviving the European Middle Ages, before flowering again in the Renaissance, whence it comes directly to the modern West.

Ideals of war that still exist today

In this book the 'Western Way of War' is interpreted differently; not so much as an objective reality, a genuine continuity of practices, but more as a strong ideology which since its creation by the Greeks has been, and still is, frequently reinvented, and changed with each reinvention. Those who subscribe to the ideology do not necessarily fight in a very different way to others, it is just that often they genuinely think they do.

not invented

Some earlier cultures fought in ways not all that dissimilar from the Greeks. The Assyrians clearly looked for open, decisive battle in which they attempted to annihilate their opponents. Their armies were trained, disciplined, composed in part of landowners, and, in what is known as the neo-Assyrian period (934–609 BC), contained armoured infantry armed solely with a spear for close combat. In their own terms they fought for political freedom. The latter cannot be dismissed out of hand by comparison with 'Western' freedom. The concept of freedom cannot be universalized. The meaning of freedom varies not only between cultures but within them as it can hold different meanings for

meaning of freedom VARIES

different groups inside one culture, and those meanings can change over time.

they just didn't make it up even though they think they did

It is far from clear that the classical cultures were as distinctive in their war-making as they liked to believe. In the 1920s an archaeological excavation of a tiny bog at Hjortspring on the island of Als in Denmark uncovered a magnificent boat and weaponry. The finds were probably deposited in the bog about 350 BC as a gift to the gods. It is likely that they were part of the equipment of a force defeated in a local war. The weaponry included swords and mailcoats, with a large number of spears, javelins, and shields. Modern interpretation has seen these finds as implying that this barbarian force, created far away from Greece and Rome, was made up of landowners, with political rights as their community understood them, organized in units of similarly equipped spearmen who used shock tactics to try to achieve a decisive result in battle; just like contemporary Mediterranean armies, especially the Roman legion of this era.

→ evolved w/out western connection

Long after the end of the classical world, other cultures would evolve a style of battle remarkably similar to the 'Western Way of War' with little or no influence from the West. As we will see, in the early 19th century in southern Africa, the Zulus changed their military organization, tactics, and equipment to create an open, pitched battle fought hand to hand by infantry, the aim of which was a decisive result.

→ SOMETIMES they actually avoided battle...

In reality the classical cultures did not always fight in the 'Western Way of War'. For long stretches of their history the Greeks actually seem to have been rather good at avoiding battle. In the 27 years of the bitter Peloponnesian War (431–427 BC) between Athens and Sparta and their respective allies, there were only two, or maybe three, significant land battles that approximate to the 'Western' style. Similarly, the Romans were not always dead set on fighting pitched battles themselves. Recalling the imperial prince Germanicus from campaigning beyond the Rhine in AD 16, the emperor Tiberius thought that Roman aims were better served by encouraging the Germans to turn on each other. In 48 BC, when the civil war between Julius Caesar and Pompey came to

→ strategy

Dyrrachium in Greece, the initial attempt to produce a result was through field fortifications rather than open battle. In AD 83, at the battle of Mons Graupius, the general Agricola drew up his army to fight the Caledonians with his auxiliaries in the front line and his Roman citizen troops to the rear. Writing this up, his son-in-law Tacitus claimed that the victory would be vastly more glorious if no Roman blood were shed.

↳ NO BLOODSHED

One factor that may encourage us to overemphasize the distinctiveness of Greek and Roman battle must always be kept in mind – that is, the types of available evidence. While archaeology can tell us a lot about their opponents, in almost all cases our literary evidence comes from the classical cultures. Had their opponents taken to comparable literary production, and had it survived, our impressions might have been very different.

Consider our evidence

The links between reality and ideology are always complex. On the one hand, the ideology of the 'Western Way of War' has shaped how reality has been interpreted. As we will see, in the 7th century AD the inhabitants of the eastern Roman empire still held that they fought in an open, 'Western' way, and that their Arab opponents did not, when in reality their armed forces went to considerable lengths to avoid pitched battle. Again, when Europeans learnt about the Zulu war machine, it was assumed that the Africans could not have created it on their own initiative, but must have copied Western models. On the other hand, the ideology can mould reality. There may have been few land battles in the Peloponnesian War, but in the opening years of the conflict the ideology meant that the Spartans marched into Athenian territory expecting to fight. If Tiberius had judged that there was the possibility that a decisive battle could have been fought in Germany in AD 17, he probably would not have ordered Germanicus to return Roman forces to the banks of the Rhine. The siege works at Dyrrachium did not settle the issue between Caesar and Pompey; that was achieved on the battlefield of Pharsalus. Tacitus might claim a victory without Roman blood as an ideal, but the legionaries at Mons Graupius were willing and able to fight.

Reality vs. Ideology

more as an **IDEOLOGY**

Although the links between the two are far from straightforward, it is best for us to interpret the 'Western Way of War' more as an ideology than an objective reality. To do otherwise, to think of 'Western War' as a continuous practice, is to homogenize history. It can lead all too easily to thinking that there has always been just one 'Western Way of War', and probably by extension just one 'Other Way'. This would iron out the differences between past and present and between different cultures, and the differences between ourselves and the people of Greece and Rome are as interesting as the similarities. It might be that we learn more about ourselves when we are rather surprised to find these differences than when we just see ourselves reflected back.

Re-reading the book to write this preface, I feel that the need for brevity has led to the 6th century AD, which saw the wars of reconquest waged by the emperor Justinian, and recorded by one of the last great classical historians Procopius, being given short shrift. To remedy this in some measure, I have included some modern works on this period in the further reading section of the book. The latter should be thought of almost as an eighth chapter, and the relevant sections be read in tandem with the main text, as it puts my arguments in the context of modern scholarly interests and debate, and enables the reader to take his or her interests further.

① How?   ② ideology?

The book looks at both how war was done and, the far less studied topic, how war was thought about. It tacks between using specific pieces of evidence to build general observations, and analysis of some particular examples of the big themes and controversies of modern scholarship, thereby hoping to encourage readers to do similar history for themselves in other contexts.

The pleasant task remains for me to thank here various people who have helped me with this book: George Miller, editor and friend, for first commissioning it, and for clarifying various ideas in discussion; then, for constructive criticism, two colleagues and friends, Maria Stamatopoulou at Lincoln College, Oxford, and Michael Whitby at the University of Warwick; and the anonymous reader for the Press.

Finally, I would like to dedicate the book to the memory of my father, Captain Hugh Sidebottom, who on 3 September 1939 volunteered to fight in a war.

List of illustrations

The publisher and the author apologize for any errors or omissions in the above list. If contacted they will be pleased to rectify these at the earliest opportunity.

List of maps

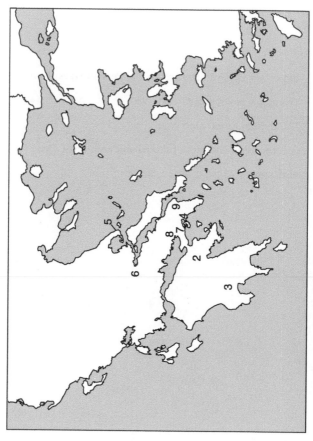

1 Troy
2 Mycenae
3 Sparta
4 Athens
5 Artemisium
6 Thermopylae
7 Salamis
8 Plataea
9 Marathon

1. Important places in the Trojan and Persian Wars

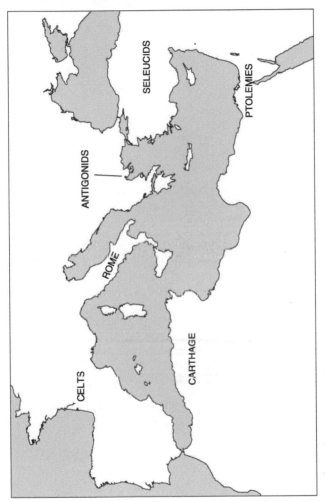

2. The major powers, c. 270 BC

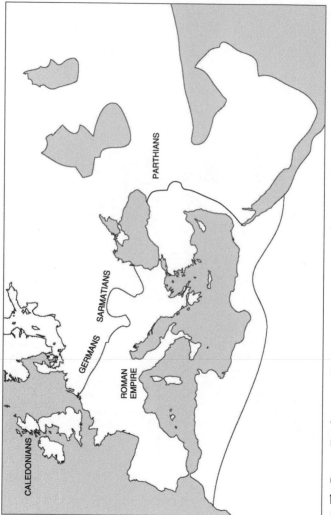

3. The Roman Empire, AD c. 117

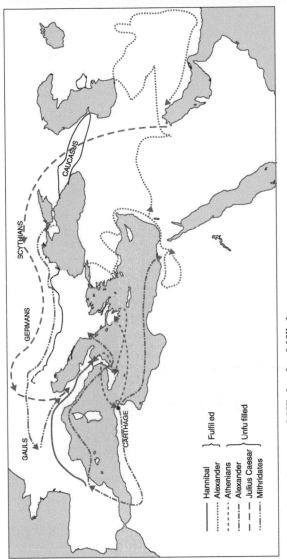

4. Great plans of conquest, fulfilled and unfulfilled

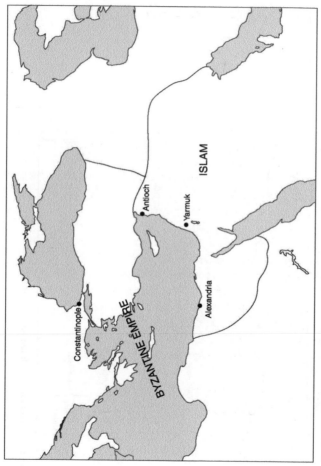

5. Arab conquests, AD c. 640

Chapter 1

'At my signal unleash hell': the Western Way of War?

"western way"

The film *Gladiator* opens with an epic battle in the forests of Germany. On one side are the Romans, in disciplined units with uniform equipment. They wait in full view, in silence, and prepare their relatively high-technology weapons. Their watchwords are 'strength and honour'. As orders are issued from a set hierarchy of command, they shoot as one, and advance in line. In combat they help each other, and display courage. On the other side are the barbarians. They have no units, and, clad in furs, no uniformity. Some carry stolen Roman shields, but they lack the catapults that represent the top level of military technology. Initially they conceal their force in the woods. Surging backwards and forwards, each man clashes his weapons on his shield, and utters wild shouts. Their yells are just gibberish. The only indications of hierarchy are close-ups of a particularly large and hairy warrior. They rush into combat as a mob, and fight as ferocious individuals.

civ. vs. savage

On one side is civilization, on the other savagery. The Romans are portrayed as practising what is often described as the 'Western Way of War', where the aim is an open, decisive battle, which will be won by courage instilled in part by discipline. The Germans practise a 'skulking' kind of war. They aim to ambush. They fight without discipline, but with an irrational ferocity. Viewing the battle, it seems 'true' to us, because it seems 'natural'. Yet it is not 'natural'.

no discipline

1

The 'Western Way of War' and its opposite are cultural constructions. It is important to ask where this concept of a 'Western Way of War' originated, why it was constructed, and why maintained.

[handwritten: ↓ culturally constructed war methods ↑]

Greeks and Trojans

We can begin by thinking about Homer's *Iliad*, the first work of Western literature. This Greek epic poem is set in the mythical time of the Trojan War, c. 1200 BC, when a coalition of Greeks, led by the king of Mycenae, besieged and sacked the city of Troy in Asia Minor. The poem began its life then, but told and retold by generations of poets, and altered in the retelling, it reached its final form in the 8th or 7th centuries BC, finally being written down in the 6th century BC.

[handwritten left margin: retold]

[handwritten: Greeks led by king Mycenae — sacked Troy]

Some elements of the poem might suggest that the idea of a 'Western Way of War' is present already: that the Greeks practise it, and the Trojans do not. More Trojans die than Greeks, and they suffer more horrific wounds. Certain verbs of pain are only applied to Trojans. The Trojans in the poem speak in less assertive and warlike tones than the Greeks. Only Trojans beg for their lives at the point of a spear. Twice we are told explicitly that the Greeks help each other in battle. Again twice, we read that the Greeks advance into battle in silence, unlike the Trojans who bleat like sheep, or sound like wildfowl.

[handwritten: → Western way belongs only to Greeks]

In all probability, however, a 'Western Way of War' in the *Iliad* should not be constructed out of all this. The Trojans' less martial language can be explained because they are at home, defending, and often speaking to, their parents, wives, and children. The Greeks are in an armed camp, comprised only of warriors, and their spear won female captives. More Trojans die because ultimately they will lose. The Trojans begging for their lives, suffering more horrific wounds, and having verbs of pain applied to them all serve to increase the pathos of the fate

[handwritten bottom: War planned out vs. attacking defending at home]

2

which every reader knows is coming to Troy. Just three passages (3.2–9; 4.428–38; 17.364–5) in a very long poem account for the two explicit statements of Greeks aiding each other in battle, and advancing in silence. In contrast, one passage tells of the Trojans advancing in silence (13.41). In the course of the narrative Trojans, as well as Greeks, come to the aid of their comrades.

In general this Greek epic telling part of the story of a mythical Greek triumph over non-Greeks, is remarkably free of xenophobia. The Greeks are not privileged over the non-Greeks. The Trojans, and their allies, and the Greeks share social and political structures. Both sides live in cities, ruled over by kings, with councils of elders, and general assemblies. They have the same equipment for war: chariots, helmets, bronze armour, shields, spears, and swords. Some on both sides use bow and arrows. They employ this equipment in the same ways: fighting sometimes at a distance, sometimes hand to hand; sometimes individually, and sometimes as a group. Above all, they share the same motivation. The poem puts its finest speech detailing the heroic code which motivates men in 'hot battle' into the mouth of Sarpedon, a Trojan ally from Lykia in Asia Minor.

> it is our duty in the forefront of the Lykians to take our stand, and bear our part of the blazing battle, so that a man of the close-armoured Lykians may say of us: 'Indeed, these are no ignoble men who are the lords of Lykia, these kings of ours, who feed upon the fat sheep appointed and drink the exquisite sweet wine, since there is indeed strength of valour in them, since they fight in the forefront of the Lykians.

> – now, seeing that the spirits of death stand close about us in their thousands, no man can turn aside nor escape them let us go and win glory for ourselves, or yield it to others.'

> (12.315–28, tr. R. Lattimore)

3

Compare Sarpedon's speech with that of a Greek hero.

> Now Odysseus the spear-famed was left alone, nor did any of the
> Argives [Greeks] stay beside him, since fear had taken all of them.
>
> And troubled, he spoke then to his own great-hearted spirit:
>
> 'Ah me, what will become of me? It will be a great evil
> if I run, fearing their multitude, yet deadlier if I am caught
> alone –
> Yet still, why does my heart within me debate on these things?
> Since I know it is cowards who walk out of the fighting,
> But if one is to win honour in battle, he must by all means
> Stand his ground strongly, whether he be struck or strike down
> another.'
>
> (11.401–410, tr. R. Lattimore)

In the *Iliad* there is no 'Western Way of War' that marks the Greeks
out from their enemies.

↳ Greeks don't "stand out"
w/ this ideology

Greeks and Persians

Although Greek poets of the Archaic period (776–479 BC) did make
the occasional disparaging remark about foreigners, the way of
thinking about the world that divided it into superior Greeks and
inferior barbarians came about with the Persian Wars (490–479 BC)
and their aftermath. It was with the creation of this dichotomy that
the concept of a 'Western Way of War' was born.

By the time of the Persian Wars most of the Greeks lived in a large
number of autonomous 'city states' (*polees*, singular *polis*). After a
great wave of colonization (c. 750–550 BC) these had spread
beyond the Greek homelands of mainland Greece, the Aegean
islands, and the western coast of modern Turkey to the west
(Sicily, southern Italy, and the Mediterranean coasts of France
and Spain), and the shores of the Black Sea, as well as a few

settlements in North Africa. Each *polis* [← city-state] lived under its own laws, and a greater or lesser number of its adult male citizens controlled its political life. The core of the military forces of a *polis* was a citizen militia, mainly comprised of farmers. These fought as hoplites: heavy armoured infantry, organized in a close-packed phalanx, equipped only to fight at close quarters with a thrusting spear and sword.

Twice, in 490 and 480/79 BC, forces of the Persian empire, which had already won control of the Greek *polees* of Asia Minor, and some of those of the Aegean islands, invaded mainland Greece. Persia was a young and expansionist empire. Its armies consisted of more or less useful levees from its subjects, and a core of Iranians. The latter included both horse and foot. They had the capacity to fight both at a distance (with bows and javelins) and hand to hand (with spears and swords). The first expedition, a relatively small-scale affair by Persian standards, was defeated by the hoplites of Athens, with a small contingent from Plataea, at the battle of Marathon. The second invasion, led by the Persian king in person, was on an altogether grander scale. Not all the Greeks of the mainland joined a league to oppose it. In 480 BC a small Greek force, led by 300 Spartans, was overwhelmed at Thermopylae, despite heroic resistance. At the same time a naval battle off Artemisium ended in a draw. Later that year the Greeks won a naval victory at Salamis. The following year the Greeks decisively defeated the Persian army at the battle of Plataea.

The Greek victories must be considered surprising. They were outnumbered. Their hoplite phalanxes were a simple instrument compared with the flexible Persian forces. The Persians had defeated other Greek forces on previous occasions.

Apart from specific tactics and circumstances, Herodotus, [→ historian] the great Greek historian of the Persian Wars, accounts for the result at Plataea thus: 'in courage and strength they (the Persians) were as good as their adversaries, but they were deficient in armour, untrained, and greatly inferior in skill'. In his narrative the Persians fight bravely hand to hand until they are demoralized by the death of their commander. Herodotus was a moral relativist. The stated aim of his history was to preserve the deeds of both Greeks and barbarians. For him, barbarians usually form a contrast to Greeks in their habits. But that did not make the barbarians worse than the Greeks. Except in one way. Greeks lived in political freedom, while barbarians, under their kings, lived in political servitude. Herodotus' attitude was not to be the prevailing one in the aftermath of the Persian Wars, when the Greeks, led by the Athenians, went on the strategic offensive.

Thought Greeks >>> bc barbarians = no freedom politically

A more typical Greek attitude can be found as early as 472 BC, when Aeschylus' play *The Persians* was performed at Athens. The scene is the Persian court, as it waits for, and then gets, news of the defeat of Salamis. Asia is depicted as rich, fertile, luxurious, and essentially female. Greece, by contrast, is rocky, rugged, and masculine. The Persians fight for their king, who is cruel, sacrilegious, and cowardly. They are servile: prostrating themselves, and afraid to speak before even the ghost of one of their rulers. They are emotional: giving way to immoderate grief. The Greeks fight for freedom. In Persia the king is the state; in Greece it is the men who form the *polis*. Many Persians are named, but no Greeks. This gives the impression that the Greeks are communal in a way that the Persians are not. Again and again the Persians are labelled as horsemen and bowmen. The Greeks, in contrast, are spearmen, as shown in the following extract of dialogue between the Persian Queen Mother (significantly, a woman) and the Chorus of (significantly) old men.

> Queen: Have they [the Athenians] such rich supply of fighting men?
> Chorus: They have: soldiers who once struck Persian arms a fearful blow [i.e. at Marathon].
> Queen: Are they skilled in archery?

Chorus: No, not at all: they carry stout shields, and fight hand to
hand with spears.

Queen: Who shepherds them? What master do their ranks obey? *free*

Chorus: Master? They are not called servants to any man. *men*

Queen: And can they, masterless, resist invasion?

Chorus: Yes! Darius' vast and noble army they destroyed [i.e.
Marathon again].

(pp. 235–44, tr. P. Vellacott, slightly altered)

The downgrading of Asiatics is yet clearer in a work by an unknown
Greek of the 5th century BC preserved in the writings of the medical
author Hippocrates.

> The small variations of climate to which the Asiatics are subject,
> extremes both of heat and cold being avoided, account for their
> mental flabbiness and cowardice –
>
> – such things appear to me to be the cause of the feebleness of the
> Asiatic race, but a contributory cause lies in their customs; for the
> greater part is under monarchical rule.

(*Airs, Waters, Places*, p. 16, tr. P. Cartledge)

The Persian Wars fixed the ideology of a 'Western Way of War'
firmly in place. The Greeks fight for freedom. They seek open battle,
which they will fight hand to hand, and win because of their
training and courage. The servile Persians fight at the command of
an autocrat. They are effeminate cowards, because as bowmen they
seek to avoid close combat, and as horsemen they are quick to run
away.   NO BIAS – just IDEOLOGY!

This, of course, is not an unbiased analysis, but a strong ideological
construct. In the wars the Persians had sought open battle, which,
as Herodotus tells us, they had fought hand to hand with courage.
Herodotus reminds us that not all Greeks at all times subscribed to
the dominant ideology. Some Persians were seen by Greeks as brave
men. Persians as a whole could be seen as representatives of an

not everyone agreed

ancient, wise culture. After the wars the Greeks adopted various Persian material goods. Part of the definition of a culture is that it allows its members to hold views which are logically incompatible.

Romans and Carthaginians

The concept of the 'Western Way of War' was to prove remarkably durable, adaptable, and exportable especially to Rome. From the start, Rome was exposed to a certain level of Greek influence. By 270 BC Rome ruled the Greek cities of southern Italy. The First Punic War (the conventional name for Rome's wars with Carthage, from 'Poeni', the Roman name for Carthaginians), 264–241 BC, ended with Roman control over many Greek cities in Sicily. The Second Punic War, 218–201 BC, brought Roman dominance over the western Mediterranean. The Third Punic War, 149–146 BC, resulted in the destruction of Carthage.

Roman society and organization under the Republic was structurally extremely aggressive. Elite desires for glory and gain, desires agreed to by the non-elite, fuelled expansion. So did Rome's control of its Italian allies. These were not taxed, except for providing troops for Rome's armies. The main weapons of the city state of Rome were the legions, a citizen militia of heavy infantry, mainly composed of propertied farmers. At one time these had been armed as hoplites, but by the Punic Wars were equipped with *pila* (heavy throwing javelins) and sword.

Carthage was a city state in North Africa, founded in the 8th century BC by Phoenicians from the Near East, who, by the First Punic War, had built an overseas empire comprising parts of Sicily, Sardinia, the Balearic islands, and areas of Spain. Having lost its Sicilian and Sardinian territories in the aftermath of the first war with Rome, Carthage expanded the areas of Spain under its control before the second war. By the time of the Punic Wars, Carthaginian forces, although commanded by Carthaginians, were not composed of citizens of Carthage. Instead, Carthage used subjects, allies, and mercenaries, all of whom were allowed to fight in their native styles. The Carthaginian style of war-making facilitated the Roman portrayal of them as being 'eastern', and not fighting in the 'Western Way of War'.

In representing the Carthaginians as 'eastern', cowardly barbarians, the Romans seem to have made relatively little use of Carthage's genuine eastern origins. Possibly the Romans' own mythical origins as Trojans from the east precluded pushing this line too hard. Instead, geography and climate served. Living in a trading seaport made the Carthaginians greedy and mendacious. For Romans, treachery was one of the marks of a Carthaginian. Punic 'good faith', *Punica Fides*, meant the opposite. Also, they were cruel and superstitious. These traits came together in their human sacrifices, above all of their own children. Carthage was feminized. Carthaginian women were dangerous seducers, like the mythical Queen Dido. Carthaginian men were effeminate, wearing loose, unbelted clothes, and lacked control of their sexual appetites. Getting others to do their fighting for them showed their cowardice. In Roman eyes, this could be explained by their living in Africa. It was considered that the hot sun meant that Africans had little blood in their bodies, and so, fearing to lose what little they did have, they were scared of wounds, and thus were cowards. A final 'proof' of their barbarity, their otherness, was that they were believed to eat dogs.

The negative ethnographic image of the Carthaginians was constructed partly out of reality (they did sacrifice some of their children), and partly out of fantasy (they almost certainly did not eat dogs). It was maintained in the face of contrary evidence. Carthaginian armies sought open, decisive battles against Roman armies, and, led by Hannibal, often won them. This could be explained away. The Carthaginians had relied on the courage of others to fight their battles, and it was the supreme cunning of Hannibal that had won them.

As we have seen, the Greeks can be said to have had a love-hate relationship with Persian culture, perhaps with the stress on the latter. The same is far less true of the Romans and Carthaginian culture. When they destroyed Carthage, the Romans gave away its libraries to 'African princes', with the exception of a practical work on farming which was translated into Latin. Probably via the army, the odd word of Punic (such as *mapalia*, huts) found its way into Latin, maybe with the adoption of the item described. Punic culture and language were not suppressed. By the time Carthage existed only as a re-founded city of Roman citizens, a writer of geography in Latin could point with pride to his Punic world view, and as the historian Tacitus pointed out in the early 2nd century AD, now it did not matter if you praised Rome or Carthage. Yet the ethnographic stereotype remained. It comes as no surprise that the first Roman emperor to have Punic ancestry, Septimius Severus, was widely seen as cruel, superstitious, and cunning.

Didn't really hate eachother anymore

Romans and Greeks

BUT ETHNOGRAPHIC BIAS caused issues later

The final shift of the boundaries of who was considered to fight in the 'Western Way of War', and who was considered 'eastern', and thus did not, that we will consider in this chapter involves heavy irony as we turn to the Roman conquest of the Greek world.

On his death (323 BC), Alexander the Great of Macedon ruled both Greece and the old Persian empire. His successors fought to carve up his empire. Out of a maelstrom of intrigue and war, three long-lived and stable 'superpowers' emerged by the 270s BC. These were the Macedonian-ruled 'Hellenistic' kingdoms of the Antigonids (centred on Macedonia, and dominating Greece); the Selucids (based in the Near East, and controlling parts of Asia Minor); and the Ptolemies (whose main power base was Egypt). During the 2nd century BC Rome defeated both the Antigonids and the Selucids. After three wars and a revolt, Macedonia was made a Roman province in 147 BC. The following year Greece was incorporated into the province of

270s BC   ① *Macedonia*   10   ③ *Ptolemies*
② *Selucids*

Ancient Warfare

Macedonia. After a war against Antiochus III (192–189 BC), the Selucids were expelled from Asia Minor, and became clients of Rome. A Roman province of Asia was created in 133 BC, when the last ruler of the kingdom of Pergamum in Asia Minor left his domain to Rome in his will. In a series of battles the Roman legions had comprehensively beaten the Macedonian-style armies of the Hellenistic monarchs, which were based around a pike-armed phalanx.

Rome took all of it & defeated everyone

In the 2nd century BC, at the very time that they were conquering the Greek east, the Romans began to take on a very large amount of Greek culture; the process we know as Hellenization. These two factors are connected. As we have seen, Rome was exposed to Greek influences from the beginning, and had ruled Greek cities from the start of the 3rd century BC. But it was in the 2nd century that Rome penetrated mainland Greece, the home of the Athenians and Spartans, who had greater cultural prestige for the Romans than did the Greeks of Italy and Sicily. Also, it was in the 2nd century that Romans, above all elite Romans, began to win vast sums of wealth from their conquests, and wealth was very necessary for the Hellenization of Rome. The Roman elite was deeply internally competitive. Hellenization offered a new way for members of the elite to compete with each other; as, for example, they rivalled each other in owning more Greek art. Hellenization served other uses for the Roman elite. It marked them off from the Roman non-elite, who could not afford to buy into the game, and it linked them to allied Italian elites, who did have the wherewithal. Art and architecture were given new trajectories, and literature and philosophy kick-started from cold. By the next century, no area of Roman elite life was unaffected. The Roman elite educated their sons in Greek. They had Greek architects design their buildings, and Greek artists decorate them. At home they often dressed in Greek costume, and spoke Greek. The Greek *symposium* (dinner/drinking party) became their social gathering of choice. It seems that no high-status Roman home was complete without a tame Greek intellectual.

Hellenization

Greek influence on ELITE completely

in every aspect have could have more Greek. Wherever was superior

Still didn't respect the ppl.

Becoming Hellenized did not mean that Romans necessarily approved of, or liked, the Greeks they conquered, and then ruled. An ancient Greek referred to himself as a *Hellene*. The Romans did not extend that courtesy. Instead, a Roman would call a Greek a *Graecus*. This was known to be offensive. Far more offensive was *Graeculus*, 'little Greek' (a Carthaginian likewise could be called a *Poenulus*). This may have had similar connotations to a white man in the southern states of America calling a black man 'boy'. Romans could consider that the Greeks of the distant, classical past, well before the Romans fought them, had been good men. Possibly they had even been much like Romans. But their descendants were degenerate. They were avaricious and corrupt. Lying was in their nature. Some Greeks were worse than others. Those from Asia were naturally servile. The Latin satirist Juvenal wrote angrily of Greeks coming to Rome (3.58–125). Especially he detested Greeks from Syria: 'the shit from the River Orontes was flowing into the Tiber' (3.62–6). Yet all Greeks could be thought luxurious, licentious, and effeminate. The very cultural products that elite Romans were taking to in such a thoroughgoing way were objects of suspicion. They might be considered to undermine the very 'manliness' of a Roman. Philosophy could be thought to make a man unfit for a life of action. The naked athletics of the Greek gymnasium was held to encourage immorality; in fact, homosexual sex was claimed to be a Greek import via the gymnasium. Pliny the Younger complained that in his day physical instruction was no longer the province of old soldiers with military decorations, but *Graeculi* (*Panegyric* 13.5). Greek athletics was not a good training for war, and war was crucial to the Roman construction of a negative stereotype of Greeks.

Roman opinion

In Roman eyes, the Greeks were no good at war. As Tacitus showed, you could give them Roman military organization, arms and equipment, as well as Roman citizenship, but they remained Greeks: lazy and undisciplined (*Histories* 3.47). Above all, they were cowards. If you found a brave one, as did the author of *The Alexandrian War* (15.1), you had to compare him with Romans, not other Greeks. The Latin poet Lucan put a savage denunciation of

Some Greeks worse than others

Ancient Warfare

abt Greeks in nature

12

the Greeks into the mouth of Julius Caesar. They were over-educated, luxurious, soft, lazy, and scared of their own shouting (*Pharsalia* 7.400–410). An anecdote the Romans told about Hannibal implies a lot about their attitudes to Greeks and war. When in exile in the Greek city of Ephesus, the great Carthaginian general listened to a philosopher lecture on generalship and military affairs in general. After the performance, which went on for some hours, the Greek audience was enthusiastic in its response. When Hannibal was asked what he thought of it, he said he had listened to many old fools in his time, but never as big a one as this (Cicero, *On Oratory* 2.75–6). FOOLS

Various factors facilitated the Roman conception of the Greeks as cowardly and 'eastern' at war. The first Greeks the Romans ruled were those in Italy and Sicily, and they had long been held by other Greeks to be soft and luxurious. 'Sybaritic' behaviour came from Sybaris, a Greek city in Italy. The conquests of Alexander the Great had spread Greeks throughout the Near East. These settlers had been joined by locals who adopted Greek culture. It was just a short step to apply the pre-existing stereotypes about the natives of the Near East to the Greeks and 'culture Greeks' who lived there, and then to Greeks as a whole. The Hellenistic pike phalanxes did fight at close quarters, at a distance of some feet as their long pikes projected from their line. But this was not as close as the Romans aimed to fight, at the point of a sword. Rome as a Republic conquered the Greeks. The majority of Greek-style armies that the Romans overcame were in the employ of kings. No ancient commentator saw the Roman Republic as a democracy (although some modern scholars see it as something rather like one). Romans could find the root of Greek decline in the democracies of the classical past. In them the poor had controlled politics, and dragged the Greeks down. To elite eyes, the poor, 'scum' as the Romans called them, were as irrational and lacking in fortitude as any barbarian.

All the above helped, but the Romans mapping onto the Greeks the stereotypes of cowardly easterners, who did not fight in a 'Western Way of War', stereotypes that the Greeks themselves had invented, was ultimately caused by the brute fact that the Romans won, and the Greeks lost.

[handwritten annotation: Grks created it but Romans didn't even thrive they had it bc of who won?]

Art and the 'Western Way of War'

Art reflects thinking, but also shapes it. Many of the ideas around the 'Western Way of War' and its opposites come into focus if we look at a visual image of conflict (Figure 1).

1. A detail from the decoration on a Greek crater, a jug to mix wine and water, from southern Italy, dated about 440 BC

On our left is a Greek hoplite, the 'Western Way of War' personified; on our right, an easterner. In battle scenes in Greek and Roman art the victors usually move from the viewer's left (possibly influenced by the European practice of reading script from left to right). The westerner is naked. This is an artistic convention, usually referred to as 'heroic nudity'. It allows the artist to show the Greek's hard, muscled body: the result of tough agricultural work and/or athletic

[handwritten annotation: Heroic nudity]

[margin text: Ancient Warfare]

training. The easterner is clothed, so we cannot see if the body is soft or hard, trained or untrained. The westerner is hairy, and explicitly masculine. The easterner has no facial hair. This lack of male secondary sexual characteristics juxtaposed with the carefully illustrated male genitals of both opponent and horse creates an impression of femininity. This can lead to the figure being interpreted as an Amazon, a mythical female warrior from the east. The westerner is on foot, and stands on the base line of the scene. His right foot is even 'planted' into the base line. The easterner is on horseback, and the horse is depicted in mid-air, as its rider appears to rein it in (seemingly indicated by the taut line of the reins between bit and left hand, the open mouth of the horse, and the heavy lines of compression on its neck). The evocation is of one steadfastly standing his ground, while the other is 'flighty', and ready to run. This is reinforced by the body angles of the two: the westerner leans his upper body forward towards the diagonal made by the two weapons; the easterner leans back. There is a contrast in the ways they hold their weapons. The westerner grips his firmly, with all four fingers curled round its shaft. The easterner's grasp is looser, with only the two central fingers gripping it. They want to use their weapons in different ways: one to thrust, the other to throw. grip

→ not bad depiction
just different.

However, there are ambiguities in the picture. The easterner is not straightforwardly dehumanized or demonized. He/she has wonderful possessions: fine clothes and a magnificent stallion. The easterner's face betrays no fear. It is beautiful and calm. Significantly, there is collusion and reciprocity between the two combatants, as they look straight into each other's eyes. Midway along the locked gaze of the fighters, the horse looks out of the picture at the viewer, drawing him or her into the scene, and into an evaluation of the 'Western Way of War'.

Chapter 2
Thinking with war

War was good to think with in the ancient world. In other words, Greeks and Romans frequently used ideas connected to war to understand the world and their place in it. War was used to structure their thoughts on other topics, such as culture, gender, and the individual. War was pervasive in classical thought.

Culture

thought of east in terms of war

When Greeks and Romans thought about 'eastern' cultures, and by reflection their own culture, they often did so in terms of warfare. This pattern of thinking was not confined to delineating the oriental. It was a universal practice, although the range of other cultures imagined was limited. For example, when inhabitants of the Roman empire looked to the east, unsurprisingly they saw 'eastern' cultures (depending on their viewpoint Greek, or Persian, and so on). When they turned to the south, again they saw mainly 'eastern' cultures (Carthaginian and Egyptian). To the west was nothing except the ocean, and in it some more or less mythical islands (such as the Islands of the Blest, where a privileged few of the dead lived). It was different up north. The 'northern' was another important imagined other for the classical world. Indeed, before their Romanization, and sometimes in humour afterwards, the inhabitants of the far west, Spaniards, were considered 'northern' in character.

West + North = other
eastern = was everywhere

Let us now think about the far north, modern Scotland, and how the Romans conceptualized, and implicitly judged, Caledonian culture largely by its style of war-making. We can approach this by examining three very different pieces of evidence: a sculptured and inscribed sandstone slab, a wooden tablet with a fragment of writing on it, and a literary text. These reveal not only the diversity of sources available to the ancient historian, but also the variety of interpretations that every piece of evidence can provoke.

War-making - judged by this

In the reign of the emperor Antoninus Pius (AD 138–61) the Roman frontier in Britain temporarily moved north from Hadrian's Wall to the line of the Clyde-Forth. Here the Antonine Wall of timber and earth was built. The military units involved erected decorated stones commemorating their part in the work. Twenty of these stones, now known as 'legionary distance slabs', have been found. One of these, found at Bridgeness, and probably to be dated to AD 142/3, marked the eastern end of the fortification (Figure 2).

Slabs to commemorate war

The inscription records the completion of 4,652 paces of the wall by the Second Legion. It is flanked by two sculptured scenes. To the viewer's left, a Roman defeats local barbarians. To the right, members of the legion prepare to offer sacrifice to the gods. The hierarchy within the legion is shown, as the main figure wears a toga, while the rest wear a tunic and military cloak. The slab poses challenges of interpretation for the viewer, as he or she tries to link the different elements of the decoration. The scene of successful battle can be understood as preceding and underpinning the scene of peaceful activity: victory in war as necessary precursor to civilized life. Alternatively, the sacrifice can be seen as securing the gods' favourable attitude towards the Romans, and thus underpinning the military triumph. Again, the sacrifice can be seen as a ritual purification for tasks ahead, and thus can be linked with the inscription. Just as there is no one way to read the relations between the different elements, so the scene of fighting can be interpreted in various ways. Rather than see it as one Roman

lots of diff interpretations

Sacrifice can also mean diff things

17

2. The Bridgeness Slab

beating four Britons, it has been suggested that it shows one Briton in four chronological stages of defeat (reading the figures clockwise from the top left: knocked down, wounded, captured, and beheaded). It is possible that such readings are too specific. As the slab was set up by the whole legion, and the cavalry were only a small part of the legion, the one stands for the whole, and the Roman represents communal effort. Also he stands for civilization. He has carefully detailed 'high-technology' equipment, and his pose can be traced back to a famous funeral monument from Athens of the 4th century BC. The Britons form a strong contrast. They are naked savages. The only cultural artefacts they have are weapons of war. No social hierarchy is indicated. Although there are four of them, their very different poses suggest that they fight as individuals. They are circumscribed by Roman civilization, surrounded by a pillar of an arch to the left, the cavalryman above, and a column to the right. They have only such future as Rome allows them. For the two in the middle register it is death in battle. For the lower two it is capture, and then for one execution. The (for the moment) living captive has been interpreted variously as being stunned, resigned, contemplative, or shamed. Caledonian culture is thought about here only in terms of war, and specifically failure in war. It is interesting that these potent symbols of Roman power appear from the circumstances of their discovery to have been carefully buried when the Antonine Wall was abandoned.

The Roman fort of Vindolanda, near Hadrian's Wall, has, since 1973, yielded several hundred writing tablets. Among the Vindolanda Tablets, which were thrown away and buried as rubbish, is one dated AD c. 97–102/3. It talks about the local Britons. The six surviving lines can be translated as follows.

> the Britons [*Brittones*] are unprotected by armour [or 'naked'].
> There are very many cavalry. The cavalry do not use swords nor do
> the wretched [or 'little'] Britons [*Brittunculi*] mount [or 'take up
> fixed positions'] in order to throw javelins.

(Number 164)

It has been interpreted as an intelligence report, or a memorandum for a new commander referring to enemy tribesmen. Alternatively, it has been seen as a report on new local recruits to the Roman army. It is just possible that it is part of a literary composition. Whichever is the case, British culture again is judged solely in terms of war-making, and is found wanting. Here many fight as cavalry, but not in the way Romans do. The Britons fail to mount (or take fixed positions) to fight. They do not fight hand to hand. They have a low cultural attainment. They are unarmoured (or naked), and they do not have swords. They are referred to by the patronizing and dismissive *Brittunculi,* 'wretched'/'little' Britons.

While it may be thought unsurprising that British culture is analysed only in terms of war in evidence coming from the very frontier of the empire, and produced in specifically military contexts, the same cannot be held of our third piece of evidence, Tacitus' *Agricola*. This hagiographic life of Tacitus' father-in-law is notoriously hard to fit into any ancient genre of literature. Probably written in AD 98 in Rome, it has in it elements of biography, history, geography, ethnography, and political treatise. As Agricola was governor of Britain AD 77–84, the ethnography given is of the Britons (Sections 11–12). This opens with a discussion of what the physical characteristics of the various British tribes shows about their geographic and racial origins. The Caledonians' red hair and large physique points to their German origins. Like the Gauls, the Britons are quick to face danger, but then quick to run away from it. Those Britons who were conquered early by the Romans have less spirit than the rest. Then their tactical methods are outlined. Their strength is infantry, but some also employ chariots. The noblemen drive the chariots, their dependants fight in their defence. Nothing has aided the Romans as much as the British tribes' inability to unite. Again, when a Roman wants to discuss British culture, it is done mainly through ideas of war. War was always one of the most important ways of comprehending the differences between cultures.

When the Greeks and Romans constructed an ethnographic stereotype of the 'northerner', they did so to form a contrast not only from themselves, but also from their image of the 'easterner'. While easterners were small, decadent, clever, and cowardly, northerners were big, primitive, stupid, and (at least initially) ferocious. Both, of course, lacked the rationality, self-control, and discipline of the classical viewer. Yet as with the easterner, the image of the northerner could be turned around. As we have seen, easterners could be regarded as having an older civilization than the classical. For the northerners, their very primitiveness could be used to depict them as uncorrupted by a civilization that had slid over into decadence. Tacitus' work of ethnography, the *Germania*, in large part can be read as a condemnation of contemporary Rome by comparison with noble Germans.

Northerner and easterner did not exhaust the classical ethnographic imagination. The other great stereotype constructed was the nomad. Nomads could be found in the north (Scythians and Huns, among others), the east (Arabs and Saracens), and the south (Libyans and Moors). Lacking agriculture and houses, let alone cities (the key signifier of classical civilization), nomads were considered the polar opposite of Greek and Roman culture. As such, although there were exceptions (for example, Quintus Curtius 7.8.12–30) and they could be thought of as having produced the odd wise man, such as the Scythian Anacharsis, they were seldom held up in classical literature as embodying a good alternative lifestyle.

These stereotypes proved remarkably durable. That the Greeks and Romans liked to think that their enemies remained the same, while in reality they changed, can be illustrated by thinking about the German tribes that Rome faced in the 1st century AD and those of three centuries later. By the 4th century AD the Germans were organized in fewer and larger tribes than they had been earlier. An intensification of agriculture had fuelled both population boom and economic growth. German society had seen increases in political centralization and social stratification, with the emergence of relatively stable dynasties of monarchs, and the appearance of a warrior elite, which can be seen as a 'nobility in the making'. These might be thought likely to have increased the coercive powers available to the tribes, and thus also to have improved the command and control that could be exercised in battle. Germanic armies may have been larger, and better equipped, with more cavalry and bowmen. Yet our Roman literary sources make these speculations hard to verify. For them, a German remained ever a German. This comes out clearly if one compares Ammianus Marcellinus' late 4th-century account (16.12) of the battle of Strasbourg in AD 357 with Tacitus' early 2nd-century description (see especially 2.14) of campaigns in Germany in AD 14–16 in the *Annals*. The two historians concur on many things. The Germans have large bodies that tire easily. They fight with undisciplined ferocity, which then gives way to complete panic. Ammianus' picture of close combat is a timeless expression of Roman ideology.

> [The Germans] had the advantage of strength and height, the Romans of training and discipline. One side was wild and turbulent, the other deliberate and cautious. Our men relied on their courage, the enemy on their prodigious physique.
>
> (16.12.47, tr. W. Hamilton)

Here changes in either Roman armies or their opponents are for the most part written out of history.

For Greeks and Romans, not only did barbarian peoples tend to remain the same, but newly encountered tribes promptly were equated with those previously known. When the Huns burst into the Roman world in the late 4th century AD, Ammianus admitted that he could find out little about their origins, and called them by their contemporary name. Yet even he drew upon earlier literature about other peoples to write his description of them. Other writers, especially Greeks, went much further, identifying the Huns with a range of barbarians that had been known in the distant past of the 5th century BC or even earlier. They were Scythians, Massagetae,

Cimmerians, and so on. In making these equations, the authors were attempting to show their knowledge of classical literature, above all of Herodotus, and thus exhibiting their elite social status. Underlying justifications for the practice was a feeling that the great writers of the past must have known about the seemingly 'new' barbarians, and that, as the recently encountered came from much the same part of the world as tribes already known, the former must have incorporated the latter. Above all, such a way of viewing the world acted as a 'defence mechanism', or an ideological 'comfort blanket'. New and threatening tribes became less unknown, and more manageable. They had been defeated or contained before, and they would be again.

Such ethnographic thinking was so ingrained that remarkably it survived the fall of the western Roman empire. In the 5th century AD some Roman subjects of the new barbarian kingdoms in the west used it to rewrite reality and feel better about their present political circumstances. Their new barbarian rulers were depicted as being just like Romans, if not actually Roman in origin all along. Flattered by the fiction, and possibly appreciating that it could encourage the loyalty of their new subjects, some of the barbarian rulers were also happy to buy into this strategy of thinking.

That the classical world had a restricted range of ethnographic stereotypes of alien cultures; that these were assembled out of a limited number of building blocks (big/small, cowardly/ferocious, decadent/primitive, and so on); that they were durable, transferable, and adaptable; and that they were used to define the centre (Greeks and Romans) by contrast from the periphery (barbarians) does not mean that they tell us nothing about the non-classical world. The classical world did not exist in a vacuum. There were other cultures out there. To seek to understand another culture on your own terms does not mean that you are indulging in free fiction. If classical culture had just wanted a mirror to see itself in, there would have been no need to construct more than one 'Other'.

The, to our eyes, artificial nature of classical ethnography should not lead us to assume that it was only an intellectual parlour game, which Greeks and Romans could indulge in, for example, when reading Tacitus' *Agricola*, but would have jettisoned when confronted with the reality of barbarians on a battlefield. The Romans fighting at the battle of Strasbourg, described by Ammianus (above), would have seen the reality of 4th-century AD German armies, but they would have interpreted this through centuries-old ethnographic stereotypes. To use a modern comparison, the reality of fighting other peoples on the Eastern Front in the Second World War did not shake the Nazi ideologies indoctrinated in German soldiers, rather it reinforced them.

Gender

Gender and the related area of sexuality are much studied currently by ancient historians (see Chapter 3 for speculation on reasons for changes in scholars' interests and views). Little of this work covers warfare. Yet war was strongly gendered in classical antiquity.

War was emphatically the work of men and not women. It was thought that goddesses might appear on the battlefield. In Homer's *Iliad* Athena, Artemis, Hera, and Aphrodite fight, the latter even being wounded by a man. Yet what was acceptable for divinities was not the case for mortal Greek and Roman women. This is clear in the *Iliad* in Hector's words to his wife.

> Go therefore back to our house, and take up your own work,
> the loom and the distaff, and see to it that your handmaidens
> ply their work also; let war be the care of men
>
> (6.490–2, tr. R. Lattimore, slightly altered)

Aristophanes' comedy *Lysistrata*, first performed in Athens in 411 BC, turns Greek norms upside down for comic effect. To end the Peloponnesian War the women of Athens go on a sex strike, and seize the city's war funds. It is part of this comedy of inversion that the heroine tells us that when her husband quoted Hector's line to her she ignored it, and then she goes on to state 'let war be the care of women' (lines 520–38).

It was a mark of their difference that among various barbarian peoples women played an active role in warfare. In Tacitus' *Agricola* it is part of their exotic nature that the 'Britons make no distinction of sex in their appointment of commanders' (16; cf. 31). In classical literature there is a succession of frightening, but perversely attractive, foreign warrior queens: Artemisia of Caria in Asia Minor, Olympias of Macedon, Cleopatra of Egypt, Boudicca and Cartimandua of Britain, and Zenobia of Palmyra in Syria. The ultimate example of warrior women were the mythical Amazons. They were held either to live without men, except for an annual mating with a local tribe, or, by crippling their male children, to have reduced their men to the roles normal for women in classical society. Amazons existed in myth to be fought and defeated by men. *Amazonomachies* ('battles against Amazons') were extremely popular in art, featuring in the sculptural programme of many Greek temples, including the Parthenon in Athens. These transgressors of the gender boundaries of war ultimately reasserted those very boundaries in their defeat. Usually they were located in the remote east of Asia Minor. The myths of the Amazons thus connected with classical ideas about the effeminate nature of eastern men.

We can advance our thinking about gender and war by looking at a visual image (Figure 3). This is part of the sculpted relief decoration of a tomb in Lycia in Asia Minor, dated to 390–380 BC, which is known as the Nereid Monument. It shows a fortified city under attack. Nine warriors man the battlements. They are equipped with the helmets and round shields of Greek hoplites. They hold stones to throw at the enemy. In the middle of the city is a woman. She alone looks out of the sculpture straight at the viewer, drawing us into the scene. Her right arm is folded over

Thinking with war

3. The Nereid Monument, showing the siege of a city

her head, while she reaches upwards with her left arm. What is she doing? A modern viewer might speculate that she is praying. This, however, is unlikely to have been an ancient response. Although women were important in Greek and Roman religion, they had little involvement in the rites of war.

The scene is an assault on a city. When war, as it were, came to the home, women, if they had not been sent away for their own safety, did have several roles to play. In *The Bravery of Women* by the Greek biographer Plutarch, the theatre for the display of female virtues is often a siege. Women could prepare food for their defenders, as 110 who had not been removed to Athens did in Plataea in 429 BC. After the invention of torsion artillery, they might donate their hair to make the ropes necessary for its working, as at Byzantium when it was invested by the forces of Septimius Severus in the late 2nd century AD. They might bring missiles to the walls, and encourage the men, as did the women of Chios in the late 3rd century BC. The author of a mid-4th century BC guidebook on how to defend a city under siege recommends that you can dress women as men, and station them on the battlements, to make the number of defenders appear greater. Yet on no account must you let them throw anything: 'for even a long way off a woman betrays her sex when she tries to throw' (Aeneas Tacticus, 40). A unusual myth credits the women of Argos with physically fighting off a Spartan attack on the walls of their city in the early 5th century BC. If the enemy broke into the town, women might throw tiles down on them from the roofs. It was such a missile, thrown by a poor, old woman of Argos, that felled King Pyrrhus of Epirus in 272 BC. Women needed watching in a siege. More avaricious than men, as well as less rational and brave, they might betray the town to the enemy, as the mythical Tarpeia tried to at Rome.

The woman on the Nereid Monument most likely should not be read in any of the above ways. Instead, she is tearing her hair and lamenting her potential fate. Should the city fall, her future holds rape, enslavement, violent death, or life as a refugee.

War was a crucial element in constructing masculinity in Greece and Rome. Homeric heroes encourage each other in battle with 'be men, my friends'. The Athenian orator Aeschines, defending himself in court, dwells on the war record of his male relatives and himself. Conversely he rounds on his prosecutor, Demosthenes: 'you claim to be a man, but I would not call you one, as you were prosecuted for desertion'. Rather Demosthenes is a *kinaidos*, a womanish, insatiable passive homosexual (2.148–51; 167–9). It was the lack of self-control and passivity, rather than just desire for male-male sex, that unmanned the *kinaidos*. Imagining legislation for an ideal city, Plato wishes that a man who has shown himself a coward could be changed into a woman. As that is impossible, 'we can reward him by giving him the closest possible approximation to that penalty'. He must spend the rest of his life in safety, and live with the resulting shame (*Laws*, 944A). Pliny praises the Roman emperor Trajan for putting on gladiatorial games, 'nothing lax or dissolute to weaken and destroy the manly spirit of his subjects' (*Panegyric*, 33.1). The link between war and masculinity was embedded in language. In Greek *andreia* meant manliness or courage. In Latin *virtus* signified manly virtue or valour.

The individual

War was not only good to think with for big issues, such as culture or gender, but it also was useful for the small-scale, and intimate, such as individual character. Here we will look at how members of three groups, which were in reality very unwarlike, nevertheless constructed their personalities in large part in terms of war.

Love and war had long been linked, but it was in the time of the first Roman emperor Augustus (31 BC–AD 14) that Latin poets, above all Propertius and Ovid, most fully elaborated the connection. The poet could portray himself fighting against love. Conversely he might be a soldier in the army of either his mistress, or love itself. He could campaign against rivals, or the woman's husband, or her virtue. A soldier of love, like a real soldier, had to be tough. Soldiering of either type demanded the same virtues, and ran the same risks: uncertainty, hardship, even death. The role of soldier of love could be desired by the poet, and a delight, or it could be a dire necessity forced upon him. Whichever, it involved renouncing the role of real soldier. This brings us to the first of two vital interpretative issues with this literature. Is it pro or anti the establishment?

Augustus, who had come to power via civil war, set out to create not only a new political order, although it was dressed up as a restoration, but also a new morality, which again was depicted as a return to the past. The Augustan regime put heavy emphasis on doing one's duty to the state, including in marriage, procreation, and war. The poets' rejection of real soldiering in favour of fighting for illicit, unmarried love thus flew in the face of the regime's wishes. Yet we should not simply see these poets as political dissidents. Self-deprecation and hyperbole always undercut the poets' self-presentation.

The other great question about this poetry is 'did they mean it?'. Again, there is no simple answer. You probably could have walked the streets of Rome without having to step over the prostrate, love-struck bodies of major poets. Yet even if they had claimed that the lover in their poems was just a fictional, poetic persona, their construction of their own personalities would have been formed in reaction to it ('the protagonist in my poems is a soldier of love, but I am not').

The principate (30 BC–AD 235) founded by Augustus largely banished war to the social and geographic periphery. Wars were now fought by professional soldiers, and, except for civil wars, they usually happened on distant frontiers. That Greek philosophers of the time never, or hardly ever, experienced war did not stop them pontificating on the subject. The philosophers, however, did come across soldiers. Their attitudes to the members of the army who protected them were marked by alienation, contempt, and fear. They considered that the life of a soldier was one of discipline, toil, and risk. As Epictetus (AD c. 55–c. 135) put it, if soldiers did not heed discipline 'nobody will dig a trench, or raise a palisade, or keep watch at night, or expose himself to danger' (3.24.32). Yet these were just the features which a philosopher claimed distinguished his own life. For example, Dio Chrysostom (AD c. 40–c. 112) repeatedly stressed the philosopher's need for discipline, and boasted of his own courage and the tribulations he had suffered in exile. Such things did not bring the soldier any benefits, but they did the philosopher, who had entered into them willingly, after philosophical deliberation. Philosophers depicted themselves as soldiers fighting for self-control, truth, and virtue. Dio Chrysostom claimed that the fight for virtue and against the pleasure which would undermine it was a greater fight than those in the *Iliad* (8.20–22; see Chapter 4 for more on these philosophers' views on war).

If the members of any group in the Roman empire had good reason to hate soldiers it was the Christians. Although (with the exception of Nero in AD 64) the initiative for the persecution of Christians came not from the government, but from the pagan populace, until the reign of Decius (AD 249–51), when the authorities became involved, as they had to for the sake of public order, it was the soldiery who oversaw the rounding up of suspects, their trials and executions. The strong element of paganism, and especially the cult of the emperors, in military life made it difficult for Christians to become soldiers, and for Christians to accept soldiers into their communities. It is thus unsurprising that the most common image of the persecuted in the Christian stories of martyrdom that survive (now usually known collectively as *The Acts of the Christian Martyrs*) is not of a soldier, but of an athlete. In a rare instance where we find a martyr described as a warrior of God fighting for faith, it is because he actually was a soldier (Eusebius, *History of the*

Church, 6.41.16). Yet in other contexts, away from martyr texts, even Christians could see themselves as soldiers. The Christian writers Tertullian (AD c. 160–c. 240) and Origen (AD 184/5–254/5) were committed pacifists, who held that Christians should not serve in the Roman army (see Chapter 4 for Christians' attitudes to war). For them, the battles of the Old Testament were to be read as allegories. Drawing on this, the few positive military images in the New Testament, and their knowledge of pagan Greek philosophy, they saw Christians as a new type of spiritual soldier. As Tertullian put it: 'for are not we too soldiers? Soldiers, indeed, subject to all the stricter discipline, that we are subject to so great a general [Christ]' (*On Exhortation to Chastity*, 12). Origen wrote: 'we do not fight under him [the emperor], although he require it; but we fight on his behalf, forming a special army – an army of piety – by offering our prayers to god' (*Against Celsus*, 8.73).

The use of war to construct individual personality, unsurprisingly, was not confined to unwarlike intellectuals. It was pervasive in the classical world. Its very pervasiveness sometimes seems to have been missed by modern scholars, and this has led to an over-literal reading of some evidence.

The general change from cremation to inhumation under the Roman empire in the 2nd century AD caused a boom in the production of stone sarcophagi (literally 'flesh-eaters'). Among the types of relief sculptures that decorated these were the 'battle scene', in which Romans (or Greeks) fought barbarians, and the 'clementia scene', in which a Roman general accepted the surrender of barbarians (and thus was exercising his clemency). Both scenes appear on the Portonaccio Sarcophagus (named after the place where it was found), which is probably to be dated to AD c. 180–190 (Figure 4).

The main scene on the body of the sarcophagus, on the longest of the three sculpted sides, shows an energetic battle. A commander, the focal point of the composition, leads a wedge of Roman cavalry

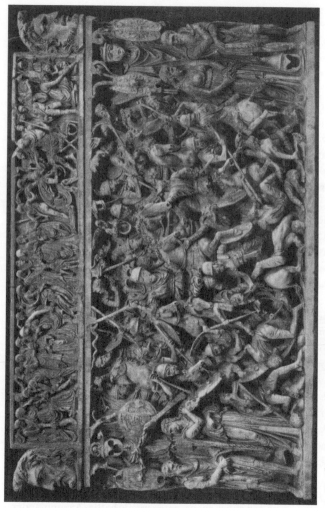

4. Battle sarcophagus from Portonaccio

into combat. Below this unit other Roman infantry and cavalry defeat barbarians. The base is carpeted with barbarian bodies. The impetus of the troopers' charge has penetrated the mass of the enemy, leaving some hostiles behind them. Yet victory is assured by the fact of the captured barbarians and trophies of arms which flank the scene. On the lid are three scenes: from left to right, a child is bathed, a wedding takes place, and a Roman general receives submissive barbarians.

Among modern art historians there seems an overwhelming desire to interpret this sarcophagus, and others like it, as more or less biographical; to assume that the deceased placed in it actually was a general. Here, as elsewhere, speculation has even named the individual. These biographical temptations are best avoided. We seldom know the immediate archaeological context of sarcophagi, or have the epitaph that once identified the deceased. 'Battle' and 'clementia' scenes were just two choices among many for the decoration of sarcophagi. Some of the other options clearly were biographical, such as a sarcophagus showing the dead man as a shoemaker. But the vast majority were not. Most depicted Greek myths, such as the labours of Hercules, or the Greek hero Meleager hunting. The ways in which sarcophagi were used points away from an automatically biographical reading. One sarcophagus was found to contain the remains of no fewer than seven adults and two children. A 4th-century AD sarcophagus with a battle scene contained a female of the imperial family, probably Helena, the mother of Constantine. Whether it was originally intended for her or not, a battle scene sarcophagus in this case was used for someone who could not have been a general.

If we look closely at the main figures on the Portonaccio Sarcophagus, the cavalry commander in the main scene, the general, the couple getting married, and the woman overseeing the bathing of the child on the lid, we can see that their faces are not finished. This suggests that the purchasers of sarcophagi did not commission them from scratch. Instead, workshops produced sarcophagi with a fairly standard range of decorations, which could then be 'personalized' for the purchaser by finishing off the main figures with portraits. We should not assume that the majority of sarcophagi with 'battle' or 'clementia' scenes happened to be bought by retired generals. These sarcophagi should be interpreted symbolically. The very high cost of a sarcophagus made a claim of elite status. If a sarcophagus featuring Hercules was chosen, it showed that the deceased wished to be seen, or his family wished him to be seen, as associated with the virtues of the civilizing mission of the hero who laboured to rid the world of monsters, and after death became a god. Similarly, if the purchaser selected one, like the Portonaccio Sarcophagus, with a 'battle' or 'clementia' scene, it showed that the deceased was to be remembered as possessing the much admired military virtues of valour (*virtus*) and clemency (*clementia*), even if in reality he had nothing to do with warfare. Some contemporaries might have gone further and seen the 'battle' as a triumph over death itself. In the commemoration of a dead individual, yet again war was good to think with.

In the late Roman empire, from the second half of the 3rd century AD onwards, more and more people conspicuously thought of themselves as soldiers. From top to bottom, members of the civil service were allowed to refer to themselves as soldiers, were in a hierarchy of ranks, wore military-style uniforms, above all the military belt (*cingulum*), and on retirement became 'veterans'. Laws were thought necessary to stop, or at least limit, the unentitled from wearing military kit (*Theodosian Code*, 14.10.1 [382]). It was always good to think with war in the classical world.

Chapter 3
War and society

It is well known that the way in which a society makes war is a projection of that society itself. To give an example. The early 19th-century rise of Zulu desire for decisive battle, fought hand to hand, and resulting in the slaughter of enemy combatants and the incorporation of everyone else into the Zulu state was caused in large part by the rise of autocratic Zulu kingship, which sought to focus all political loyalty on the person of the king via the army.

This chapter looks at things the other way round. It takes three examples that, it has been argued, illustrate that war-making profoundly changed Greek and Roman society.

The 'hoplite revolution' in Greece

A way of approaching the military aspect of the supposed 'hoplite revolution' in the Greek world of the late 8th and/or 7th centuries BC is to look at two ancient visual images of fighting. The first is a late Geometric, c. 735–720 BC, oinochoe (wine jug) from Athens (Figure 5).

The style of fighting appears fluid and individualistic. Some warriors are mounted on chariots, others are on foot. One of a pair of warriors, often identified as the mythic siamese twin sons of

5. Oinochoe (wine jug) from Athens, c. 735–720 BC

Actor, moves to mount a chariot. The 'twins' have a square shield, others an oval with semi-circular cutouts at the sides (often referred to as a 'Dipylon' shield after the cemetery in Athens where many pots depicting such shields were found), while others have no shield. Fighting seems to proceed via throwing spears and close-quarter work with swords.

The fighting shown on this pot can be interpreted as matching closely the fighting depicted in Homer's *Iliad*, in which it can be thought individual heroes, riding in chariots, and dismounting to fight, first by thrown spears, then with swords, dominate the battlefield, while the mass of their followers usually are reduced to spectators or victims.

The second image is on the famous 'Chigi vase' (named after a former owner). The top figure scene on this Protocorinthian, c. 650 BC, olpe (jug) shows men in battle (Figure 6).

Here the style of fighting appears cohesive and communal. The warriors are arranged in serried ranks, and move in step. All are armed alike, with a round shield, and are about to fight with a thrusting spear.

The fighting shown on this pot can be interpreted as being the same as, or very close to, what became the distinctive Greek style of fighting later in the 5th and 4th centuries BC; the hoplite phalanx,

6. Chigi vase from Corinth, c. 650 BC

which we know from the historians Herodotus, Thucydides, and Xenophon. The hoplite phalanx consisted of heavy infantry, organized in a close-packed 'shieldwall' several ranks deep, all carrying round shields, and fighting primarily with a thrusting spear. (We will explore the experience of this type of fighting in Chapter 6.)

It is interpretations like those above that underpin the modern theory that the Greeks significantly changed their style of war-making some time before c. 650 BC, when the 'Chigi vase' was painted. The original battlefield is seen as a 'primitive' one, akin to those recorded by anthropologists in highland New Guinea. It is a 'place of fear' with little in the way of formations or tactics. In it individuals motivated by their personal desires to gain honour and avoid shame have a wide latitude in deciding when, where, and who to fight. As such, it is unsurprising that a small number of aristocrats decide the day. They have more to gain and lose in the honour/shame game, and have the best equipment (though few scholars would argue that they used chariots in reality). This is seen as being replaced by a 'civilized' battlefield, the key elements of which are two formations, the opposed phalanxes. Once the virtually identically equipped warriors are assigned their places in the phalanx (and it must be confessed that no one has any real idea how that happened), they have next to no choice in when, where, or who to fight. A desire to defend their community, their *polis*, now is added to personal interests as motivation to prevent them exercising one of the few choices left to them – to stop fighting, try to force their way through the ranks behind them, and to run.

This supposed military revolution has been seen as the cause of deep political and social changes. An outline of an argument by a scholar who made an important contribution provides a route into this area. Antony Andrewes argued that an increase in trade led to the creation of a new group of relatively wealthy non-aristocrats in Greek society. It was these people (principally farmers who benefited from better economic conditions) who constructed the hoplite phalanx. Once in the communal organization of the phalanx, now the main military weapon of the *polis*, this 'middle class' came to demand political rights, and thus supported, or at least did not oppose, the rise of tyrants, who overthrew the previously existing aristocratic regimes. After the fall of the tyrannies, it was the hoplites who dominated most Greek states. Although differing on many issues, such as how the phalanx was introduced (at a stroke, or gradually over time), who introduced it (rich non-aristocrats, aristocrats, or tyrants), and, above all, what the effects of its introduction were, several scholars agreed that there had been (1) a significant military reform, and (2) that this had some political and social repercussions. The 'hoplite revolution' had made it to 'orthodoxy'.

It could not last. Joachim Latacz was an early opponent of the 'orthodoxy'. In his reading, the warfare described in the *Iliad* was hoplite warfare. Few scholars have followed such an extreme line. But several have taken a 'revisionist' position. They tend to see 'proto-hoplites' on the Homeric battlefield. In their readings of the *Iliad* the impact of individual heroes is minimal, and the decisive factor is massed fighting by ordinary warriors. There is thus no room for a military 'revolution'. Instead, at most, there was a gradual adoption of new items of equipment, and a slow trend towards uniformity. With the forefathers of the hoplites already playing the vital role in battle, the final 'formalization' of the hoplite phalanx could not have inspired important political and social changes. Needless to say, not all scholars have accepted these arguments, and the 'orthodoxy' has been re-argued.

How can such opposed interpretations exist? In part it is down to our evidence. Our knowledge of Greek warfare in the 8th and 7th centuries BC is poor. Despite the enthusiastic endeavours of 'experimental archaeologists', who create and use replicas, finds of weaponry tell us less than we might expect. We can never be certain that an item of kit was used in the most 'sensible' or 'rational' way.

Let us turn to supposed 'pre-hoplite' warfare, and look again at the Athenian oinochoe illustrated (Figure 5). Was the artist trying to give a realistic picture of contemporary warfare, and would contemporary viewers have tried to see it in those terms? What about the chariots, for whose use in war at this time there is no archaeological evidence outside art, or the 'Dipylon' shields which are only found in art, or the possible presence of Siamese twins on a battlefield? Much the same questions can be asked of Homer. While clever readers of the *Iliad* can make the warfare in it appear coherent, does that mean we have anything more than a coherent poetic or fictional world? We know that items of equipment in the *Iliad* come from widely separated periods of Greek history; Mycenaean 'tower shields' jostle with what sound like contemporary hoplite shields. Might not the tactics also be an amalgam of different periods?

In a similar way, our grip on early hoplite warfare is slight. Poets of the 7th century do not always seem to describe hoplite fighting. Callinus of Ephesus talks of fighting with javelins, not thrusting spears (fragment 1). Tyrtaeus of Sparta in one fragment (11) gives what we think of as a classic description of a close-packed hoplite phalanx. Yet the fragment ends (line 35) with *gumnetes*, the 'naked' (lightly armed), crouching under the shields of the hoplites.

Look again at the scene from the Chigi vase, and imagine what would happen to the action in a moment's time. The front ranks are poised for the killing blow. All four on the left will fall, as will four on the right. This will leave one warrior on the right, and the flautist on the left isolated between the second ranks. Or will it? If you look closely at the painting, you can see four warriors in the front rank on the left, but ten legs. Most warriors carry a second spear, which later hoplites did not, and many of these spears have a loop to aid throwing, whereas later hoplites thrust their spears. The ranks are not packed close behind one another, as most believe later hoplites were. If we did not know about hoplite battle in the 5th and 4th centuries BC, would we automatically interpret this scene as representing a clash of phalanxes several ranks deep?

There is a serious danger of taking what we know of later hoplite fighting, altering it, and retrojecting it into the past. We take the densely ordered phalanx of the 5th and 4th centuries BC, strip it of its supporting light troops and cavalry, as well as its relatively sophisticated tactics, project it onto the 8th and 7th centuries BC, and thus create a simple and 'ritualistic' phase of early hoplite war.

Given the challenges of interpreting the meagre evidence that we have, it is completely unsurprising that widely differing and opposed theories can be held about the nature of war in the Archaic Greek world, and its impact on society. The Greek hoplite phalanx was a phenomenon of the Greek *polis*. Every *polis* we know about ended up using them, and Greeks who did not live in a *polis* did not. Similarly, tyrants seem to have been a phenomenon confined to the *polis*. We do not hear of tyrants among Greeks who did not live in a *polis*. The connections between *polis*, tyrants, and hoplites remain agreeably open to reinterpretation.

What can be stated with confidence is that between c. 735 and c. 650 BC the Greeks changed how they thought about war. In this period the practice of burying men with weapons ended, except in remote areas. Again in this period the Greeks start to dedicate in sanctuaries both arms and armour, and miniature images of equipment and warriors, the most striking example of the latter being the tens of thousands of miniature models of warriors that have been found in the temple of Artemis Orthia in Sparta. Finally, around 650 BC there is an explosion of images on pots of men in hoplite equipment.

The 'Agrarian Crisis' in Italy

It is commonly held that large-scale warfare in the last two centuries BC caused an agrarian crisis in Italy, which in turn largely

43

undermined Rome's Republican government, and led to its replacement by the monarchic system we know as the principate. A neat way into this 'traditional view' is offered by the flow-chart created by ancient historian Keith Hopkins (Figure 7).

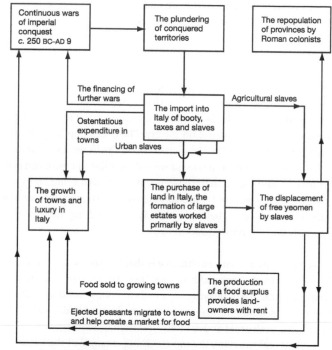

7. **Model of the 'agrarian crisis' in Roman Italy**

Let us follow the main lines of the model. The key 'motor' of the process is the top left box, continuous wars of imperial conquest. This leads to the plundering of conquered territories, the proceeds of which are imported into Italy as booty, taxes, and slaves. These (moving to the box below) fund the creation of large landed estates, which are worked primarily by slaves. The setting up of these (moving to the box on the right) entails the displacement of free yeomen (perhaps 'peasants' has less anachronistic overtones). The dispossessed peasants drift off either (following the two downward arrows) to the growing towns of Italy, above all to Rome, where they help form a market for the produce of the very estates that have replaced them, or to the army where they contribute to the wars of expansion which started the whole process. The peasants of Italy in effect were fighting for their own displacement. The 'vicious circle' finally came to an end in the reign of the first emperor Augustus (31 BC–AD 14), with the end of continuous expansionist war-making, the establishment of a professional army, and the implementation of a massive programme of settling Italian veterans in overseas provinces (top right box).

Elegant and evocative as it is, the flow-chart is a severely restricted synopsis of Hopkins' arguments. It was (as is implicit in the flow-chart) the Roman elite who got the lion's share of what was extracted from conquered territories. The highest social order in Rome, the senators, who were politically active landowners, got their cut, in the main booty and graft, via high military commands and provincial governorships. Some members of the second highest order, the equestrians, who were also landowners but less overtly involved in politics, acquired their share by tax collection and business activities. The elite did not just purchase land in Italy to create their estates. Peasant families were ejected from their smallholdings by force. The elite also enclosed public land (*ager publicus*). This indirectly removed peasants from the countryside. Peasant holdings tended to be so small that access to public land was necessary for their sustainability.

Classical beliefs that citizenship was legitimated by military service, that those who had a stake in the community were more likely to be loyal to it, and that farmers made the best soldiers explain why, probably until 107 BC, there was a property qualification to serve in the Roman legions, and that the vast majority called up were peasant farmers. In the 2nd century BC Rome's big overseas wars meant that large numbers of Italian peasants were away from their farms for long periods of time. When they returned they found that their families had been forcibly thrown off their land, or that they had entered into debts which could not be serviced, or that they were denied access to necessary public land by enclosure. Many thousands would have become casualties and either not returned at all, or been injured to such a degree that they could no longer work as farmers.

The mass eviction of peasants is thought to have profoundly undermined the Roman Republic in two ways. First, many moved to Rome, where they formed part of the ever-growing disaffected urban poor. The very real discontents of the urban plebs (*plebs urbana*) allowed some senators, often themselves from the most aristocratic of families, to set themselves up as popular politicians (*populares*), who by championing the interests of the poor gained positions of great influence, and in so doing fatally fractured consensus politics among the elite. The first open break came in 133 BC when Tiberius Gracchus, as one of the Tribunes of the Plebs, forced through a scheme to redistribute *ager publicus* to landless Roman citizens. Our sources tell us that a major motive for his action was concern at the dwindling number and reluctance to serve of those available for recruitment into the army. Second, the pressure of military service on the declining number of landed peasants led to the abandonment of the property qualification. This is usually dated to 107 BC, and linked to the actions of Marius, one of the consuls of that year. Subsequently unpropertied legionaries obviously had no farms to return to after their service, so they began to look to their generals to force the government to find land for them on discharge. At the same time, the generals began to look to their troops to support them in politics. This reciprocity of interests between legionaries and their generals would eventually bring down the Republic, as armies were prepared to follow their commanders against the state.

This 'traditional' understanding of the 'agrarian crisis' recently has been repeatedly challenged by some scholars. We will look at two of the main lines of these 'revisionist' attacks here. First, it has been suggested that warfare in the 2nd century BC was not all that different from the 3rd, and that if it had been going to cause an agrarian crisis it would have done so earlier. Second, it has been argued that our archaeological evidence does not support the 'traditional' view.

Any arguments based on the demography of Republican Rome must be recognized as tentative. Our evidence is patchy and hard to interpret. Totally opposed conclusions can be reached: the citizen population of Italy was either in sharp decline or was rising fast. In some senses warfare in the 2nd century imposed less strain than it had in the 3rd. In the 2nd century the Romans never had to field at one time the number of troops that they had for the war against Hannibal (the Second Punic War, 218–201 BC), and wars were now not fought on Italian soil. But other factors had changed. Rome now had to keep permanent garrisons in some provinces: in Spain (and possibly Cisalpine Gaul, as northern Italy around the Po valley was called) throughout the century, and in Macedonia from 146 BC. Legions in theory were disbanded every winter and new ones enrolled the following year. It was impractical to release all the soldiers serving in Spain and take a new draft out from Italy annually. Legionaries were therefore enrolled not for a set period of time, but for the duration of a campaign. If called up for service in a 'garrison' army, that 'campaign' could seem never-ending. Legionaries in such armies could be away from their farms for years at a time. The actions of Tiberius Gracchus in 133 BC were an attempt to solve a problem that had been long in the making. In the 140s BC there had been such a strong perception of a crisis that even a politician of a staunchly conservative frame of mind had proposed reform. Although, as a reactionary hero, Laelius had won the nickname *Sapiens* (the 'wise') for then dropping the whole idea.

It has been argued that the archaeological evidence that we have does not support the 'traditional' picture of an agrarian crisis in

Italy. For example, one of our main literary sources (Plutarch, *Ti. Gracch.* 8.7) says that Tiberius Gracchus was inspired to attempt reform on a journey through Etruria in Italy, when he saw the scarcity of free men, and that agricultural work was conducted by slaves. Yet archaeological survey of this region seems to show a landscape full of small farms rather than large estates. As he was a politician, it is easily accepted that Tiberius Gracchus exaggerated and generalized. But we should not assume that archaeologists automatically are immune from such behaviour. The vast majority of Italy has not been surveyed. The limitations of archaeology should be kept in mind. Often it is good at telling us how land was used (for example, to grow olives or grapes), but seldom can it tell us of the status of those cultivating the land (owner-occupiers, tenants, or slaves). The very poor, such as agricultural slaves, leave few traces, and thus are under-represented in archaeological surveys.

We must be careful not to create too rigid a dichotomy between the 'traditional' view and the 'revisionist' ones. No 'revisionist' would claim that no peasants were thrown off the land. Equally, no 'traditionalist' holds that all peasants were evicted. It is a debate about degree, not of kind. Various factors ensured that large estates could not take over all Italian land. Climate, topography, and soil were suitable for large estates only in certain areas; vines and olives flourished in western coastal Italy, pasture in the south. Unlike subsistence peasant farms ('sufficers'), estates run as profit-making businesses ('maximizers') need access to markets. Bulk transport by land was economically inefficient in the ancient world. Large estates thus were limited to areas of proximity to their markets (towns), or water transport (navigable rivers or harbours). The need for labour on estates varied during the year: large numbers of workers were needed in harvest time, far fewer in mid-winter. It would be uneconomic for an estate to keep enough slaves to cover the peak times. Instead, they kept the minimum number of slaves, and hired in extra labour for busy times. It was thus in the interest of the large estates to ensure that some peasants remained on the land in their vicinity to be employed as occasional wage labourers. Large estates never became dominant in agriculture in Italy (in the sense of farming the majority of the land), but they did become the distinctive type of farm. The replacement of peasant farms by largely slave-worked estates was enough of a perceived problem for politicians of such different views as Tiberius Gracchus and Lealius to consider that a remedy was necessary.

The 'barbarization' of the Roman army

There is a popular view that the 'barbarization' of the Roman army led to the fall of the western half of the empire. It runs something like this. During the 4th century AD the large-scale replacement of indigenous units with barbarian units, commanded by their own tribal leaders and fighting in their native styles, and the influx of barbarian officers and men into regular Roman units, which adopted barbarian equipment and fighting techniques, combined to make the empire's army less efficient, and more prone to desertion and treachery. In the 5th century AD 'barbarization' was curbed in the eastern half of the empire, but increased in the west. The east thus survived, while the west fell.

The concept of 'barbarization' recently has been the subject of repeated revisionist attacks. It has been suggested that only one in four of those officers and men in regular units about whose origins we can make a guess were barbarians, and that this number did not increase during the 4th and early 5th centuries. Also it has been argued that when whole regular units were raised from one barbarian tribe, these did not keep any corporate barbarian identity for long as replacement troops were not drawn from the original ethnic group. Similarly, it has been suggested that service in the regular army would lead to an individual recruit replacing his identity as a barbarian (Frank, Goth, or whatever) with that of a Roman soldier. On our available literary evidence it appears that barbarians in the army were no more liable to treachery or desertion than indigenous troops. It is pointed out that the Roman army had always adopted equipment and practices from its opponents, and that it is hard to see how some of those adoptions that we know from the late empire (such as wearing trousers or using the *Barritus*, a Germanic war cry) could have impaired efficiency. A contemporary commentator could claim that some borrowings from the barbarians had actually improved the performance of Roman troops. Vegetius (1.20) claims that copying from barbarians has been beneficial to the Roman cavalry.

The revisionist arguments, of course, are not above criticism. We have indications of ethnic origins for only a small percentage of officers, and a miniscule percentage of the rank and file. We are very seldom told the origins of an individual, and thus usually have to draw an inference from his name. As the revisionists admit, this is a very uncertain method. We know that some barbarians adopted Roman names, while some recruits from within the empire carried local names (Celtic, Thracian, or whatever), which can easily be taken to be barbarian. The model whereby a recruit neatly replaces his former identity with that of a Roman soldier can be doubted. A veteran described himself as '*Francus civis, Romanus miles*', a Frank ('citizen') and a Roman soldier (*ILS* 2814). There was a contemporary perception that the army had been taken over by barbarians. In the 4th century 'Goth' was a colloquialism for 'soldier' in the Syriac language spoken in some eastern parts of the empire. Some contemporaries in certain circumstances could condemn the 'barbarization' of the army. Famously, Bishop Synesius of Cyrene in the early 5th century savagely criticized the emperor Arcadius for employing large numbers of barbarians in his forces (*On Kingship*, esp. 1091). The revisionist position assumes that barbarian 'allies' serving under their own officers and in their own style had no 'knock-on' effect to the regular army. It could be imagined that the effect of serving alongside units with looser discipline and a less committed attitude to training might have been deleterious to regular units. Finally, it must be remembered that the revisionist arguments are of relevance to a limited time; only up to either the great Roman defeat by the Goths at Adrianople in AD 378 or to c. 425. In the west by the mid-5th century, Roman field armies were thoroughly 'barbarized'. In AD 451 the 'Roman' army that defeated Attila at the battle of Chalons was, depending on how one interprets our sources, either composed totally of barbarians, or the effective part was barbarian.

The revisionist arguments have shown that the 'barbarization' of the army will not do as a monocausal explanation of why the western Roman empire fell in the 5th century AD and the east survived. Other explanations must be explored: these include the west suffering both greater barbarian pressure and more usurpers of the imperial throne; its longer frontiers; lack of a virtually impregnable strategic capital like Constantinople; poorer tax base; failure to curb large landholding aristocratic families and to create a bureaucratic 'service aristocracy' akin to that in the east; and its failure to integrate army commanders into the imperial court. Yet some will still conclude that the 'barbarization' of the army had a role to play in the fall of the west.

Why do historical interpretations change?

The way in which the three sections of this chapter are structured, a 'traditional' interpretation, followed by a 'revisionist' one, then a critique of aspects of the latter, illustrates that all historical interpretations are provisional and part of an ongoing process. There are many reasons why that should be so, three of which will be picked out here.

The discovery of new material is an obvious, although much less common than might be imagined, stimulation to new interpretations. Archaeological discoveries in Italy were a factor in reassessing the 'agrarian crisis' of the late Republic.

General shifts in thinking, or intellectual fashion, influenced by changes in current political or social circumstances, often provoke new interpretations of well-known bodies of evidence. The 'barbarization' of the late Roman army was first seriously studied by

German scholars in the last quarter of the 19th and first half of the 20th century. Given the search for a corporate identity for the new German empire of the time, it is no surprise that these scholars tended to maximize the Germanic nature of Roman antiquity, and were predisposed to find a very 'Germanized' Roman army. As another example, it can be speculated that the turning against the traditional view of the 'hoplite revolution' was part of a general revulsion in the 1970s and 1980s against social-determinist, and above all Marxist, theories of historical change.

The final explanation offered here is rather more cynical: every generation rewrites history because it wants to get published and wants a job. Historians are trained to criticize the interpretations of others, and they do not, or should not, make a career rehashing the views of others. This, as one ancient historian put it, 'is normal, cyclical, endogenous change, as a new generation of historians inevitably seeks to make "progress" in understanding and explaining the past by rejecting the dominant paradigms of its mentors'.

Chapter 4
Thinking about war

After 9/11 the one remaining superpower declared a 'war on terrorism'. A manifestation of this has been two largely 'conventional' wars which have resulted in 'regime change' in two countries, Afghanistan and Iraq. Warfare, in its different forms, is something that affects everyone now, and something we all need to know about. Thinking about the morality of the then forthcoming war in Iraq, the eminent philosopher Richard Sorabji considered the views, among others, of Plato, Aristotle, Cicero, and early Christian thinkers. The thinkers of the classical world were much concerned with war, and their ideas on the causes of war, its justifications, and its acceptable limits, the subjects of this chapter, not only tell us about the past, but can inform modern discussions and attitudes.

Classical Greeks

The great historians of classical Greece, Herodotus and Thucydides, each took a war as their central theme: respectively the Persian War (480–479 BC) and the Peloponnesian War (431–404 BC). They analysed the causes of these wars. For Herodotus, revenge, kinship, and obligation were key motivating forces in history. To explain how the Persians of Asia came to fight the Greeks of Europe first he canvassed a series of mythical wrongs done by either side. Deciding that he could not judge the truth or falsity of these myths,

Herodotus chose to begin where he claimed his own knowledge started.

Croesus of Lydia (in Asia Minor) decided to attack the new power of Persia. With the defeat of Croesus (547 BC), the Greeks of Ionia (now the Aegean coast of Turkey) came under the rule of Persia. When the Ionian Greeks revolted (499–494 BC), their kinsmen the Athenians aided them. This prompted the Persian expedition to Marathon (490 BC), and defeat there caused the main invasion of 480–479 BC. Herodotus gives various reasons for Croesus' action which starts the whole chain of events. One level of explanation is human, including Croesus' desire both for a pre-emptive strike and revenge for Persian treatment of his brother-in-law. The other level is divine. It fulfils a divine promise of revenge on the Lydian royal house. The two levels are not seen as contradictory, but complementary.

Thucydides downplayed the role of the divine in his history to just *Tyche*, chance or fortune. In his analysis of the causes of the Peloponnesian war, Thucydides famously distinguished between the publicly expressed causes of complaint and the 'truest' reason, the growth of Athenian power and the fear this caused in Sparta. Although rather different from those looked for by modern historians, the analyses of the causes of these specific wars given by Herodotus and Thucydides are plausible and sophisticated. Neither, however, is particularly concerned with the justice of the wars they narrate, or offers any explicit discussion of the causes of war in general.

We might expect to find more general discussions of war in the works of the philosophers Plato and Aristotle. They concerned themselves with war, discussing who should participate in war, their education, the strategic site and defensive works of the ideal state, and its military command and organization. They did discuss problems of justice *within* warfare, such as the rewards and punishments due to one's own combatants, and the treatment of the enemy. Yet neither produced an extended or systematic discussion on the justice *of* war. The nearest they came were their infamous views on Greeks fighting barbarians, based on the ethnographic stereotypes we explored in Chapters 1 and 2, and these received just a summary outline. For Plato in the *Republic* (469b–471b), wars between Greeks and barbarians were natural, while those between Greeks were not. As such, restraint should be exercised in the latter, but not the former. Greeks should not enslave each other, and this would encourage them to turn on barbarians. Aristotle in the *Politics* (1333b38–1334a2) claimed military training had three objectives: to prevent those being trained becoming slaves, to win a leadership which would serve the interests of those being led (that is, other Greeks), and to enslave those who deserve to be slaves (that is, barbarians). The latter glances back to the opening of the *Politics* where Aristotle had worked out his theory of natural slavery.

Partly from the prescriptions of the philosophers, and partly from the narratives of historians, we can form an impression of what constituted the norms of acceptable behaviour in war. Sanctuaries and internationally recognized festivals (such as the Olympic Games) were meant to be inviolate. Yet pragmatic reasons could over-ride the ideology. Sanctuaries contained wealth and were often tactical strong-points. Only heralds appear almost always to have enjoyed immunity. It was widely accepted that prisoners of war could be ransomed or enslaved. Whether it was acceptable to put prisoners to death was more debatable. After the sack of a city, the conquerors were completely within their rights to kill the men, and enslave the women and children. Killing the non-combatants, however, was morally dubious.

The idea of just and unjust wars seems to have been common currency in Greek political discourse. For example, the orator Isocrates advised the Cypriot king Nicocles never to fight unjust wars (*To Nicocles*, 24). Yet what made a war just or unjust was seldom elaborated. A 4th-century dialogue featuring Socrates, which in antiquity was ascribed, probably wrongly, to Plato

(*Alcibiades*, 1), held that an unlawful war was one that was fought when the enemy had done no wrong. The sort of wrongs that might make for a just war were deceit, violence, or spoliation. It is to be noted that the wrong committed does not have to be a real or potential attack. Deceit is a wrong. In classical Greek thought, unlike in most modern theories, just wars do not have to be wars of self-defence.

The failure of the Greeks to produce extended and systematic theory on the just war might suggest that they thought war was the normal state of humanity, and thus did not call for elaborate theorizing. In the *Laws* Plato makes one of the speakers hold just that position: 'what most people call "peace" is nothing but a word, and in fact every city-state is at all times, by nature, in a condition of undeclared war with every other city-state' (626a). But Plato introduces this argument into the dialogue to demolish it. The character who speaks it mocks the ignorance of the majority because they hold the opposite view (625e).

The Greeks' lack of extensive theorizing on the justice of war probably did not stem from a belief that war was the normal state of affairs. Instead, the need for an elaborate ideology was weak because the causes of war were thought to be self-evident, were widely agreed, and were thought to be inherent to humanity. Most Greek authors agreed that the causes of war were the desire for profit, the pursuit of honour, and self-defence. As Thucydides made the Athenians say, it was all down to security, honour, and self-interest (1.76.2; and look again at the passage of Aristotle's *Politics* above). The causes of war thus were unproblematic for the Greeks. Equally, as there was no time limit on pointing to wrongs done, and all Greek cities were enmeshed in webs of kinship and alliance, a reason for a just war was usually to hand. The enemy, or their allies, had at some point committed a wrong towards your own people, or their allies. Such a claim need have involved no hypocrisy on the part of those invoking it.

Republican Romans

With the Romans of the Republic we seem to find systematic and formalized thinking about the 'just war'. In the process of acquiring a large and stable empire, above all after their conquest of the Greek east in the 2nd century BC, the Romans came to feel the need to justify their possession of such a power, and thus of the wars that had won it. Our best evidence comes from a fragmentary work by Cicero, but, as we will see, the views expressed probably are not atypical.

In book three of his *Republic*, Cicero wrote that the ideal state should not undertake a war unless to keep faith (*fides*), or for its safety/health (*salus*, 3.34). In another passage it was stated that a just war must have a cause, either revenge or defence (3.35). These should not be interpreted as justifying only wars of self-defence, or defence of allies. They are included, but the statements imply much more. *Fides* included a commitment by Rome to defend her allies. But the concept went both ways: the allies should keep faith with Rome. From the 2nd century BC onwards, Romans thought of all their allies as subservient, what we would call 'client states', and any people who had had diplomatic dealings with Rome could be thought to fall into this category. Failure by an ally to comply with the wishes of Rome constituted a breach of faith, and thus Roman 'revenge' would be a just war. It did not end there. Any injury to Rome, not only an attack on it or its allies, could call for revenge. A hostile attitude, or even the mere existence of a foreign power, could be considered a threat to the *salus* of Rome, and thus Roman aggression could be a just war.

In another passage preserved from the *Republic*, Cicero said that no war was just unless it had been declared (*denuntio*), a formal warning given (*indictio*), and reparations demanded (*rerum repetitio*). Here the reference is to the rituals of a Roman college of priests called the *Fetiales*, who were in charge of declaring war. Although we cannot be sure when they were founded, or how

57

continuous was their existence, the *Fetiales* did reveal Roman attitudes. The Romans believed that in their original form the rituals consisted of the three stages which Cicero gives in reverse chronological order; the demand for reparations coming first. The rituals imply that the other side has committed a wrong towards Rome (how else could reparations be demanded?), but not necessarily that this has been an attack on Rome or an ally. Also, it is Rome that sets the level of reparations to be paid, and these could be set at a level that it was known the other side could not meet. Rather than as a strong break on aggressive war-making, these rituals should be seen as a formalized way of putting the dispute before a tribunal of the gods. The gods' verdict came in the outcome of the war. If the victor was Rome, then the war had been just. After victory Rome often forced the vanquished to reimburse the costs of the war. By so doing the other side was made to acknowledge that Rome's cause had been just.

Civil war

The threat of civil war was ever present in the classical world, and it posed severe ideological problems. As Herodotus put it (7.102.1), Greece and poverty had always been foster-sisters. The unequal distribution of limited resources and the resulting division of the population in all Greek cities into a large number of the 'poor' and a much smaller group of the 'rich' meant that there was always potential for what the Greeks called *stasis* (civil strife or war). During the 5th century BC *stasis* became politicized into conflict between those who favoured government by the many (democracy) and those who desired rule by the few (oligarchy). From the Peloponnesian War (431–404 BC) onwards, there was an increased readiness both for politicians within cities to call for outside intervention in times of *stasis* and for external powers to answer these appeals. Athens, and later Thebes, tended to favour democrats, while Sparta, and later Macedonia, normally backed oligarchs.

Our best evidence for an outbreak of *stasis* in a Greek city is Thucydides' account (3.69–85) of events in Corcyra (Corfu) in 427 BC. The *stasis* escalated from disputes in the law courts. In this case it was the oligarchs who first resorted to violence, but it was the democrats who carried out the worst atrocities.

> There was death in every shape and form. And, as usually happens in such situations, people went to every extreme and beyond it. There were fathers who killed their sons; men were dragged from the temples or butchered on the very altars; some were actually walled up in the temple of Dionysus and died there.
>
> (Thucydides 3.81, tr. R. Warner)

Thucydides wrote up these events at length not so much because of their intrinsic importance, but more because the *stasis* at Corcyra was the first big outbreak during the Peloponnesian War, and thus he could use it as a peg on which to hang general reflections on the phenomenon. As the passage quoted above partially shows, Thucydides thought that *stasis* involved not just political breakdown, but also social, religious, and moral collapse. Even language changed; for example, thoughtless aggression became courage. The leaders of the opposed factions invoked admirable-sounding motives, equality for the many or sound government, but these were just covers for self-seeking. The episode was written up as a support for one of Thucydides' key themes: that the war had brutalized the Greek character. Thucydides considered that such *stasis* could always happen while human nature remained the same, but it would be less severe in time of external peace, because, in his famous phrase, 'war is a violent teacher'.

Things looked very different if you were a participant in civil war. Although its foundation myth included fratricide, as Romulus killed Remus, and after the internal conflicts which brought down the Republican form of government civil war haunted the Roman imagination, Rome during most of its history was rather better than Greek cities at avoiding civil war, possibly in part because of its relentless militarism towards other powers. Yet at times civil war was a real as well as ideological threat. The years 63 to 62 BC saw the 'conspiracy of Catiline', which ended in armed conflict. We have better documentation for this episode than for most, but ironically this makes evaluation all the harder. Our main source is Cicero, and he claimed for himself the role of chief opponent of the conspiracy. Even before the beginning of armed conflict, in his speeches *In Catilinam (Against Catiline)* Cicero described the conspiracy as a 'war'. The 'war' against Catiline was depicted as a war against luxury, madness, and crime (2.11). It was a war of virtue against vice (2.25). Other civil wars had been bad, but nothing compared to this one. In others the aim was a change of government, here the intention was the destruction of the state (3.24–5). Not only had they tried to recruit barbarian Gauls into the plot, but the conspirators themselves had become like barbarians: they were marked by criminal audacity (*audacia*), impious crime (*scelus*), and mad rage (*furor*, 1.31 etc.). In civil war it was necessary to show that your opponents had given up the right to be treated as fellow citizens; instead, being like barbarians or even worse (3.25), they deserved to be declared enemies (*hostes*) of the state. To fight another Roman it helped if you could show that he was not a Roman at all!

About twenty years after the conspiracy, the Latin historian Sallust wrote a pair of monographs to illustrate the moral decline of Rome: the *'War against Catiline' (Bellum Catilinae)* and *'War against Jugurtha' (Bellum Iugurthinum)*. Modelling his style on Thucydides, in the *'War against Catiline'* Sallust condemned the way in which political leaders cloaked their self-interest in a language of the public good (38). For Sallust, however, it was not external war that encouraged civil war, but rather its absence. Peace and prosperity had led to first a lust for money, then a lust for power (10). This was the distinctively Roman concept of the necessity of an enemy to fear. As Sallust expressed it in the *'War against Jugurtha'* before the destruction of Carthage 'there was no strife among the citizens either for glory or for power: fear of the enemy [*metus hostilis*] preserved the good morals of the state' (41).

Greeks under Rome

The circumstances of Greek philosophers under the Roman principate were very different from those in earlier ages. They were now ruled by a non-Greek autocrat, the Roman emperor. This autocracy was stable; individual emperors might be removed, but there was no realistic likelihood of the system being changed. It claimed rule over all the world, or at least the best part of it, and, with the exception of the occasional civil war, had banished war to distant frontiers, where it was fought by professional soldiers. We have already seen one effect of these altered circumstances. While Plato and Aristotle had a respect for warriors, Greek philosophers under the principate usually regarded them with a mixture of antipathy, contempt, and fear. Views on war itself also changed. Two of these views will be looked at here.

Classical philosophers had condemned wars for glory or gain, but not ones for self-defence, and thus had never sought to deny the existence of the just war. Under the principate philosophers continued to criticize wars for self-interest or ambition. But now they went further. Both Dio Chrysostom (*Or.* 80.3) and Epictetus (4.1.171-2) denied the validity of wars fought for political freedom, which logically denies the validity of wars of self-defence, and casts into doubt the validity of any war at all. Various reasons can be given for this flirtation with pacifism. Rejecting the legitimacy of wars of self-defence might be considered easier if there is no likely chance of having to fight one. Also these men were adherents of Stoicism, the dominant school of philosophy in the principate. For a Stoic, what did not affect the inner man was an irrelevance. So war, which they believed was a disturbance of cosmic harmony caused by man's wickedness or wrong judgement (and these amounted to much the same), and its horrors, such as death and enslavement, were irrelevant to a good man. Epictetus held that death lay outside the moral purpose (3.3.15), and Dio Chrysostom wrote two orations (15 and 16) to show that 'stone walls do not a prison make'.

Given their strong metaphysical objections to war, it is a surprise to find that one of these Stoics, Dio Chrysostom in his second oration *On Kingship*, could produce a cover-all justification for war. His argument ran as follows. The king (or the emperor) rules because he has complete virtue (*arête*). The most important element of this was love of mankind (*philanthropia*), which manifested itself in his giving benefits to his subjects. Thus if the king came across a tyrant he should defeat him so that in future he could give benefits to the ex-subjects of the tyrant. Equally, he should fight any other king. The winner would be shown to have the greater virtue, and would thus give greater benefits to the ex-subjects of the defeated. Although it is obviously flawed, as it imagines wars resolved by single combat between rulers and that all wars will end in total conquest, this elegant theory was to have a long and dangerous history.

Christians under Rome

Christians have always had a problem with war. How can the bloodthirsty Old Testament be reconciled with the pacifist New Testament? As we have seen, early Christians, such as Tertullian and Origen, inclined to pacifism, allegorizing away the endless 'smiting' by God and his chosen people in the Old Testament. Not wishing to antagonize the pagan authorities, they claimed that, while they would not fight in temporal wars, their prayers for the health of the empire formed them into a spiritual army. This, unsurprisingly, cut no ice with the pagans. It was precisely the Christians' prayers to their one God, and thus not to all the others, that threatened the *Pax Deorum* (divine peace) on which the empire rested. With the conversion to Christianity of the emperor Constantine (reigned AD 307–337) everything changed. Pacifism was not a realistic option for a religion of empire.

Although it is uncertain how influential his views were with his direct contemporaries, Saint Augustine, Bishop of Hippo AD 395–430, was by far the most influential writer in the development of late antique and medieval Western thinking about war. Not knowing Greek, Augustine did not draw directly on the works of pagan Greek philosophers such as Plato and Aristotle. But, well read in Latin literature, he did use Cicero. Although, as far as we know, Augustine never produced an extended and systematic discussion of war, in passages scattered in various works he tried to show that it was acceptable for Christians to engage in warfare. He accepted from Cicero and the Roman tradition that a just war must be in response to a wrong committed by the other side (*Questions on the Heptateuch* 6.10). From Old Testament history he produced evidence that the wrong did not have to be an attack (*ib.* 4.44). For this Christian, as for pagans, a just war was not limited to one of self-defence.

Two elements in Augustine's thinking were distinctively Christian. First was an appeal to authority. While a private killing, even in self-defence, was not acceptable, it was for a soldier who had a lawful commission to take life (*Letter* 47.5).

> Since, then, a righteous man who happens to be serving under an ungodly sovereign can rightfully protect the public peace by engaging in combat at the latter's command when he receives an order that is either not contrary to God's law or is a matter of doubt (in which case it may be that the sinful command involves the sovereign in guilt whereas the soldier's subordinate role makes him innocent), how much more innocent is involvement in war on the part of him who fights at the command of God who, as everyone who serves him knows, cannot command anything that is evil.
>
> (*Against Faustus* 22.75, tr. L. J. Swift)

Here part (and only part) of the responsibility is shifted to the ruler. The implication is that if the ungodly ruler issues a command which obviously is contrary to God's law, the soldier who obeys would be guilty. Stemming from the Christian division of temporal and spiritual power, and the wars started by barbarian invaders which Augustine lived through, this appeal to authority had no echo in earlier pagan thinking on war.

The second distinctive element in Augustine's thinking is a distinction between inner disposition and outward, bodily action. It is the state of mind of the participants that is all-important: 'It should be necessity, not desire, that destroys the enemy in battle' (*Letter* 189.6). In this passage God allows war in order to bring peace, in another God sends war to correct men's morals (*City of God* 1.1), and in a third it is a greater glory to destroy wars with a word than enemies by the sword (*Letter* 229.2). Yet, if fought in the right Christian frame of mind, it could almost become a duty to fight others for their own good.

If the state observes the precepts of Christian religion, even its wars will not be conducted without the benevolent design that, after the resisting nations have been conquered, provision may be more easily made for enjoying in peace the mutual bond of piety and justice.

(*Letter* 138.14)

Chapter 5
Strategy

Strategies or fantasies?

Grand but unfulfilled plans assigned to various leaders and peoples by ancient sources offer some of our most interesting information on ancient strategy. Looking at a selection of these stories, which are usually ignored or dismissed out-of-hand by modern scholars, tells us a great deal about how the classical cultures saw the world in military terms.

In 415 BC, during the Peloponnesian War, the Athenians sent an expedition to Sicily. The biographer Plutarch (AD c. 50–c. 120) claimed that for the Athenian politician Alcibiades Sicily was just the start of a campaign of conquest that would encompass Carthage, Libya, Italy, and then the Peloponnese. In Plutarch's account this plan caught the imagination of Athenians young and old: people sat in the wrestling schools and other public places sketching in the sand the outline of Sicily and the positions of Carthage and Libya (*Alcibiades* 17). The contemporary historian Thucydides gave a different order to the projected campaign in a speech he put in the mouth of Alcibiades after his defection to the Spartans: first Sicily, then the Greeks of Italy, after them the Carthaginians, and finally the Peloponnese (6.90).

After the death of Alexander the Great, a memorandum was

produced which was said to contain his plans for further conquests: first the Carthaginians, then the peoples bordering the coasts of Libya and Spain, and back to Sicily (Diodorus 18.4). As another source elaborated it (Curtius Rufus 10.1.17–9), Alexander aimed to defeat the Carthaginians, then, after crossing the deserts of Numidia (North Africa), go to Spain, then skirting the Alps and the Italian coastline, return to Epirus (Albania). A third source said that some writers gave an even more ambitious plan: to sail around Africa, enter the Mediterranean via the Pillars of Hercules (the mountains flanking the Strait of Gibraltar), and then add Libya and Carthage to his empire (Arrian 7.1.1–3).

When he was assassinated in 44 BC Julius Caesar was about to leave Rome to campaign in the east against the Parthian empire, which was centred in modern Iraq and Iran. Plutarch credits Caesar with a grandiose scheme: after defeating the Parthians he intended to cross the Caucasus Mountains, march around the Black Sea, crush the Scythians (peoples north of the Danube) and the Germans, and thus return to Italy via Gaul (*Caesar* 58.3).

Barbarians could be thought to have far-flung ambitions. When Mithridates of Pontus (in Asia Minor) had been driven to the Crimea in 63 BC, he was held to have planned to march around the Black Sea, up the Danube, and, with some Gauls, invade Italy by crossing the Alps (Cassius Dio 37.11.1; Appian, *Mithridatic Wars* 102, 109). Ardashir, the first king of the Sassanid Persians, who overthrew the Parthians in the AD 220s, was thought by those within the Roman empire to want all the territory once held by the Achaemenid Persian empire (550–330 BC). The Sassanids thus were considered to be a threat to the Roman territories of Egypt, Syria, and Asia Minor (Cassius Dio 80.4.1; Herodian 6.2.2).

The writers who give us these stories use them to illustrate the ambition of the characters involved. It can be given either a positive interpretation, constituting a great-minded search for glory (so Arrian on Alexander), or a negative one, indicating over-reaching pride (so Curtius Rufus on Alexander). It was almost always the latter for barbarians, who were thought by their nature to be disposed to such irrational desires.

Modern scholars tend to downplay these stories; 'rationalizing' them down to a more 'achievable' scale, or dismissing them either as contemporary wishful thinking or as a later invention. Possibly modern scholars are too quick to condemn. If they had not happened, Hannibal's march from Spain to Italy, crossing both the Pyrenees and the Alps, and Alexander's conquests from Greece to India, might well have been considered mere pipedreams.

Let us look more closely at one example: Athenian ambitions in the west. The evidence of Plutarch can be considered to derive from Thucydides, and thus to have no independent value. From Thucydides passages can be used to argue for and against the reality of the plan. It is most fully explained in a speech of Alcibiades which seeks to persuade the Spartans to renew the war (6.90). Here there is every reason for Alcibiades to exaggerate. It is clear that the 'grand plan' was not raised openly in the Athenian assemblies which discussed sending the expedition (e.g. 6.16–18), or in the strategy meeting of the generals when they reached Sicily (6.48). From Sicily the Athenians actually asked the Carthaginians for aid (6.88). On the other hand, it was Thucydides' own opinion that the Athenians desired all Sicily (6.6; c.f. 6.1), and that Alcibiades aimed at Carthage (6.15). Any attempt on all Sicily automatically would have caused conflict with Carthage, which controlled cities in the island. The Athenians receiving help from the Etruscans of northern Italy (6.103) indicates the wide scale of their involvement in the western Mediterranean. In a speech which Thucydides gives to a politician in the Sicilian city of Syracuse, the Carthaginians are said to be constantly apprehensive that they will one day be attacked by the Athenians (6.34). Already in a comedy produced in 424 BC the possibility of an Athenian attack on Carthage had been mentioned, albeit with comic exaggeration (Aristophanes, *The Knights* 1302–5). It was not openly acknowledged policy, but the idea was in the air. Had the Athenian expedition met with more success in Sicily, the 'grand plan' may well have appeared attractive.

The big plans can seem more 'rational' and attainable if we think about how the Greeks and Romans imagined the world. In the schemes outlined above, certain geographic features stand out: coastlines, rivers, and mountain ranges. These point towards the way in which the ancients thought about geography. Lacking accurate topographical maps, they tended not to think, as we do, in terms of blocks of territory, so-called 'cartographic thinking', but in linear terms, such as the lines of coasts, rivers, or mountain ranges, so-called 'odological thinking'. The products of this 'odological thinking' were written and illustrated *periploi*, lists of ports and landmarks for coastal sailing, and itineraries, lists of towns and stopping places along roads and land routes. It is these that seem to have been employed in strategic planning. *Periploi* and itineraries were equally as practical and as divorced from topographic reality as the map of the London Underground.

There were, of course, ancient geographers who attempted to produce topographically accurate descriptions of the world. Three points about them can be noted here. First, although their works were to be of immense importance in early modern Europe during the 'Age of Discovery', they remained specialist literature with little broad impact in the classical world. Second, their estimates of the 'inhabited world' (in Greek the *oikoumene*, in Latin the *orbis terrarum*), in other words the known part of the world and the more or less mythical places surrounding it, were vastly too small. The Greek geographer Strabo argued that the *oikoumene* was about 8,046 miles 'long' (east to west) and about half as 'wide' (north to south). Third, as with Strabo, the *oikoumene* was thought of as an oval along an east-to-west line. Europe north of the Danube was considered to be much smaller than it is in reality (thus making the plans attributed to Mithridates and Caesar less daunting for contemporaries than for us), and the west of Africa and Europe also were vastly compressed (with attendant effects on ancient attitudes to the 'plans' of the Athenians and Alexander).

In a sense, geography was of secondary importance in classical strategic thinking. The Greeks and Romans thought of conquering peoples not places. The peoples they looked to conquer were barbarians, and, as we saw in Chapters 1 and 2, barbarians were naturally inferior. Big plans of conquest, in a small world comprised of inferior peoples, who could be reached by following or crossing the lines of certain rivers, coasts, or mountains, could seem far more achievable to the ancients than they do to our eyes.

A 'grand strategy' for the Roman empire?

In 1976 the American strategic analyst Edward Luttwak published *The Grand Strategy of the Roman Empire*. As we shall see, for various reasons, some more pertinent than others, few works have caused such controversy among ancient historians. Looking at two plans from Luttwak's book (see Figure 8) provides a good path into his ideas.

In the first model, Luttwak sets out his schematic view of the Roman empire of the late Republic and early principate (down to the mid-1st century AD). It is a 'hegemonic' empire, where areas directly ruled by Rome (Italy and the provinces) are surrounded by 'client states'. The latter take responsibility for their own internal order, deal with low-level external threats, and delay higher-intensity ones. As the Roman legions, and in the principate professional auxiliaries, are not responsible for day-to-day defence of the borders of the empire, they form a mobile strategic reserve, which is available to crush independent-minded 'clients', defeat high-intensity threats while they are still in the territory of 'client states', and pursue further conquests.

The second model gives Luttwak's vision of the grand strategy which prevailed in the empire from the second half of the 1st to the

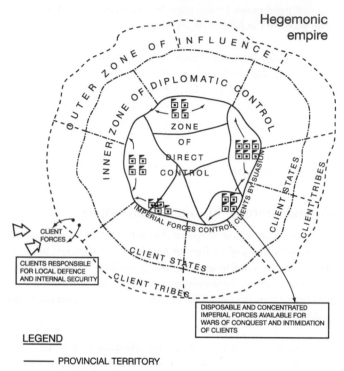

Hegemonic empire

OUTER ZONE OF INFLUENCE

INNER ZONE OF DIPLOMATIC CONTROL

ZONE OF DIRECT CONTROL

IMPERIAL FORCES CONTROL

CLIENTS BY SUASION

CLIENT STATES

CLIENT TRIBES

CLIENT STATES

CLIENT TRIBES

CLIENT FORCES

CLIENTS RESPONSIBLE FOR LOCAL DEFENCE AND INTERNAL SECURITY

DISPOSABLE AND CONCENTRATED IMPERIAL FORCES AVAILABLE FOR WARS OF CONQUEST AND INTIMIDATION OF CLIENTS

LEGEND

———— PROVINCIAL TERRITORY

—·—·— CLIENT STATE BOUNDARIES

— — — CLIENT TRIBE BOUNDARIES

▣ COMBINED TASK FORCE OF LEGIONS AND AUXILIA

8. Luttwak's two models of empire

later 3rd centuries AD. It is a 'territorial' empire. The 'client states' have gone. The legions and auxiliaries now are stationed in permanent bases along the frontiers, where they are responsible for perimeter defence. Further conquests are dangerous, as a troop build-up on one frontier involves stripping them from others. Luttwak implied that this grand strategy was a plan consciously worked out by the emperors and their advisors. It was a defensive

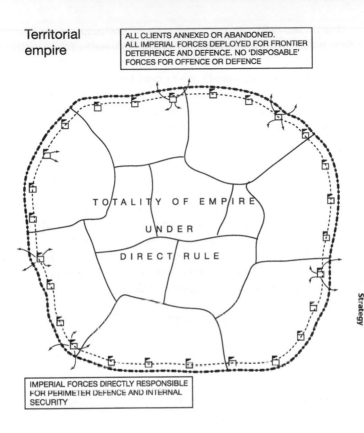

Territorial empire

ALL CLIENTS ANNEXED OR ABANDONED.
ALL IMPERIAL FORCES DEPLOYED FOR FRONTIER
DETERRENCE AND DEFENCE. NO 'DISPOSABLE'
FORCES FOR OFFENCE OR DEFENCE

T O T A L I T Y   O F   E M P I R E

U N D E R

D I R E C T   R U L E

Strategy

IMPERIAL FORCES DIRECTLY RESPONSIBLE
FOR PERIMETER DEFENCE AND INTERNAL
SECURITY

LEGEND

━━━━ GUARDED OR FORTIFIED FRONTIER PERIMETER

------ PROVINCIAL BOUNDARY

🗗   LEGIONS AND AUXILIARY UNITS DISTRIBUTED
     FOR FRONTIER DEFENCE

policy that aimed at the use of an 'economy of force', and so thought
carefully about geography, choosing good, defendable boundaries,
preferably natural (rivers, seas, deserts, or mountains) and
reinforcing them, or if necessary replacing them, with man-made
defences (walls, ditches, and cleared ground such as Hadrian's

Wall). It was defensive, but not inert. Good intelligence was to allow the Roman forces to head off threats before they reached the frontier.

Luttwak's ideas have found some support, but the majority of scholarship provoked has been hostile. It can be suspected that some of this hostility stems from the fact that Luttwak is not a professional ancient historian, and so was seen as an interloper. Certainly, Luttwak's book, with its enthusiasm for fighting wars in the territory of 'client states', made for uncomfortable reading in Western Europe during the Cold War (Luttwak was a security advisor to Ronald Reagan in the 1980s). Whatever the contemporary factors at work (and it is good to be reminded that modern historians do not work in an historical vacuum), and despite the tendency of Luttwak's critics to oversimplify his arguments (as space has forced me to do here), several telling objections have been raised against the 'grand strategy of the Roman empire'. We can look at some of them here.

'Client states' never disappeared. There was a tendency for the empire to turn existing 'clients' into provinces, especially in the east, but the Romans never ceased trying to turn peoples outside their direct control into 'client states'.

Another line of attack is conceptual. The Romans lacked the necessary mental tools to produce grand strategy akin to Luttwak's. We saw in the previous section that they lacked accurate large-scale topographic maps. Although some records were kept, treaties with foreign peoples and grants of citizenship to favoured foreigners, we can find no trace of any archive on diplomacy or foreign policy. Decisions were made by the emperors, who were expected to consult with their council (*consilium*). Yet the *consilium*, which the emperor could overrule, consisted of whomever the emperor invited to attend, and we never hear of specialists on foreign policy in specific areas or in general. The contemporary historian Cassius Dio (76.9.4) tells us that the emperor Septimius Severus was short of information when campaigning in Mesopotamia in AD 198. This was some two hundred years after the first Roman campaigns in the area.

Defensive ideals were voiced. The historian Appian in the 2nd century AD described the Romans surrounding 'the empire with a circle of great camps' (*pr.* 7). In the next century another historian, Herodian, spoke of Augustus having 'fortified the empire by hedging it round with major obstacles, rivers, trenches, mountains, and deserted areas' (2.11.5). But such statements scarcely amount to anything like Luttwak's geographically sophisticated grand strategy, and they sit uneasily alongside expressions of ideals of further conquest. Herodian also claimed that, had he not been stopped by a rebellion in AD 238, the emperor Maximinus would have conquered the Germans as far as the Ocean, and the text leaves no doubt that this would have been a good thing (7.2.9).

The Romans discussed strategy in terms that were rational for them, but can look odd to us. Cassius Dio, who had served on the *consilium* of Septimius Severus, wrote of that emperor's annexation of Mesopotamia that:

> he used to declare that he had added a vast territory to the empire and had made it a bulwark of Syria. On the contrary – this conquest has been a source of constant wars and great expense to us. For it yields very little and uses up vast sums.
>
> (75.3.2–3, tr. E. Cary)

We need not believe that Cassius Dio actually voiced these views to the emperor, but, with the exception of Severus' open vaunting of imperialism as a good thing in itself, this all seems quite normal strategic discourse to us. The same cannot be said of the reasons Cassius Dio gives for another of the emperor's expeditions.

> Severus, seeing that his sons were changing their mode of life (i.e. for the worse) and that the legions were becoming enervated by idleness, made a campaign against Britain.
>
> (77.11.1)

Campaigns and logistics: some general considerations

For a modern state, fighting a war, win or lose, is very expensive. Warfare in the classical world also could involve huge costs, especially siege and naval war. The exactions the emperor Maximinus imposed to pay for his German war led to a revolt which ultimately cost him his life (Herodian 7.3.1–4.6). Yet wars could also make huge profits. It all depended on who you were fighting and how successful you were. It has recently been demonstrated that an inscription on the Colosseum in Rome stated that it had been funded by booty. This massive project was paid for by a part of the wealth gained by the emperor Vespasian and his son Titus crushing a revolt in just one quite small province, Judaea.

One type of expense incurred in modern wars was not always present in the ancient world: paying the troops. As we have seen, in the classical city state citizenship was bound up with military service. For a long time city states thus had no need to pay their citizen-soldiers. In the Greek world the only city for which we have much evidence of military pay is Athens. There, pay appears to have been introduced in the 5th century BC as Athens acquired an empire, and at first it seems to have been a form of living allowance. During the Peloponnesian War the concept of military pay broadened to include remuneration for service, and other Greek cities began to pay their soldiers. The Romans introduced military pay during the siege of Veii, which ended in 396 BC. The emperor Augustus set up a special treasury and introduced two new taxes to pay the professional army of the principate. It is to be doubted if basic military pay was ever a road to riches. In the principate if a soldier lived long enough to collect his retirement bonus, he would be comfortably set up for the rest of his life. Otherwise, throughout the classical world, a soldier would have to look to booty for serious economic advancement.

Even some mercenaries did not need paying. Some, such as

Thracian tribesmen in the Peloponnesian War, served for free in the hope of booty. Yet most mercenaries had to be paid. Before the Peloponnesian War, most Greek mercenaries came from the poorest parts of Greece, such as Arcadia, and tended to serve either non-Greek paymasters, such as the kings of Lydia or the Egyptian pharaohs, or Greek tyrants. After the Peloponnesian War, mercenaries appear from all areas of the Greek world, and are employed not only by non-Greeks, like the Persian pretender Cyrus, the service of whose 10,000 Greek mercenaries was immortalized in Xenophon's *Anabasis*, but by Greek cities of any type of constitution. After the death of Alexander, the wars of his successors marked the high point of mercenary service in the Greek world.

Very occasionally we hear of Romans serving as mercenaries abroad (for example, one Lucius set up an inscription some time between 217 and 209 BC commemorating his service in Egypt, *IC* III 4, no.18). Yet most Romans who served foreign rulers would not have seen themselves as mercenaries. They were voluntary or enforced political exiles fighting for their restoration, as were those in the army of Mithridates of Pontus. Under the Republic, Rome, whose main strength was legionary heavy infantry, often needed additional cavalry and light infantry. Some of these were provided by mercenary service, such as the Cretan archers who fought in the Second Punic War. But, although the line between the two was blurred, the majority came from allied contingents. The professional auxiliary units of the principate removed the necessity for mercenaries, although supporting troops could still be provided by allies, and these allies might receive subsidies from Rome. The use of mercenaries revived in the late empire. In the 5th century AD prominent individuals began to hire private troops of barbarian mercenaries. Rufinus, the praetorian prefect of the emperor Arcadius, maintained a personal guard of Huns. Such troops came to be called *Bucellarii* ('military biscuit eaters'), and in the 6th century AD often formed a significant part of Roman imperial armies. By the early 7th century AD '*Bucellarii*' had become the title of a regular cavalry unit.

Logistics, the supply of water, food, firewood, fodder, and other material, were of vital importance to ancient armies, but are easily overlooked. Logistics were not often discussed in ancient literature. Normally they only got a mention when things went disastrously wrong, as when Alexander the Great crossed the Gedrosian desert (Arrian 6.22–6). Our poor evidence makes reconstructing ancient logistics especially difficult. Nevertheless, enough material can be assembled for book-length studies; particularly notable are two works on Roman logistics in general, and one on Alexander's conquest of Persia. These works have to proceed by taking logistical evidence from more recent, better-documented periods and extrapolating it backwards onto the scattered ancient evidence. This has to be done with great care. For example, estimates for the needs of modern soldiers cannot be automatically applied to ancient ones, who tended to be older, smaller, and more inured to hardship. Again, modern estimates for such things as the weights that can be carried by various pack animals vary by huge percentages. The findings of these modern studies are provisional in the extreme.

Ancient armies seldom campaigned in the winter. A winter campaign demanded special reasons. For example, Alexander's expedition against the Cossaeans of the Zagros Mountains in 324–323 BC was held to have been inspired by either the king's desire to find in action solace for his grief at the death of his friend Hephaestion (Plutarch, *Alexander* 72.3) or, the explanation preferred by most modern scholars, the strategic purpose of catching the tribe when weather conditions precluded flight uphill (Arrian 7.15). The reluctance to campaign in the winter was less to shelter the troops from bad weather, than because of the unavailability of fodder, and the difficulties of moving supplies. Water transportation was the preferred method for bulk goods in antiquity, land transportation being slow and inefficient, and sea travel was especially dangerous in winter.

Logistics become more of a problem the larger armies become, the longer they are assembled, especially in one place, and the further from home they operate.

Armies of the ancient Near East clearly had good logistic capabilities. Although Herodotus' figures must be wildly inflated (7.186), the Persian army that invaded Greece in 480 BC consisted of tens, if not hundreds, of thousands of men. Similarly, the Carthaginians by the mid-4th century BC were able to supply armies of tens of thousands of men operating abroad. Probably logistics were not usually a big problem for classical Greek armies, which tended to be relatively small, operate at no great distance from home, and not stay in existence for long. Seemingly in the normal run of things, the authorities set a date for assembly and instructed the troops to provide themselves with a certain number of days' provisions. Alexander's logistical difficulties would have been eased by his customary rapidity of movement and, after capturing the Persian treasuries, his limitless wealth. Alexander's successors and the Hellenistic kingdoms had to develop sophisticated logistic arrangements because their armies were large, often contained a high proportion of cavalry, and might stay in the field for years at a time. In 306 BC Antigonus I managed to cross the Sinai desert with an army of almost 90,000 men and a siege train (Diodorus Siculus 20.73.3–74.5).

When the Romans first fought overseas, in Sicily during the First Punic War, they had to begin to develop a high logistic capacity, based on a mixture of foraging, requisitioning, and supply lines. Although it is hard to ascertain normal practice, the Romans were capable of extraordinary feats of logistics. In the Third Macedonian War (172–167 BC) they ran a supply route for about 100 miles through mountainous terrain in the Balkans, and in AD 73/4 managed to supply a large army for a siege of several weeks, if not months, at the waterless site of the desert fortress of Masada. After their defeat of the Hellenistic monarchies, the Romans enjoyed a greater logistic capacity than any of their enemies. This advantage was noted. Cassius Dio said that the Parthians' war-making efforts

were hampered because they 'do not lay in supplies of food or pay'
(40.15.6).

Greeks and Romans liked to think of huge baggage trains as being
typical of barbarian armies. Quintus Curtius Rufus gives a splendid
description of the huge retinue, including carriages for 360
concubines, which followed the Persian king Darius III as he set out
to fight Alexander (3.3.8–25). There was an awareness of the
problems of large baggage trains. They slowed the army down, and
if they became mixed up with the troops the confusion impaired
fighting ability. The latter was held to be partly responsible for the
disaster in the Teutoburg Forest in Germany, where Varus' entire
army of three legions was wiped out in AD 9 (Cassius Dio 56.20.5).
Several famous generals, including Alexander, destroyed, or sent
away, what they considered inessential baggage. The intention in
part was to restore discipline. Scipio Aemilianus in Spain in 134 BC
'expelled all traders and whores, as well as the soothsayers and
diviners, whom the soldiers were consulting' (Appian, *Wars in
Spain* 85). When ancient sources give numbers for camp followers
or wagons, it is because they are exceptionally large. In 171 BC in a
raid the Antigonid king Perseus captured 1,000 wagons from his
Roman opponents (Livy 42.65.1–3). At the battle of Orange in 105
BC the Romans are said to have lost 80,000 soldiers and 40,000
servants and camp followers (Livy, *Periochae* 67). Modern scholars,
however, can be thought to play down the size of baggage trains in
the armies they study. For example, the major work on Macedonian
logistics accepts as both true and normal campaigning practice a
figure for camp servants that is both dubious and refers explicitly to
one training exercise (Frontinus, *Stratagems* 4.1.6).

Ancient writers tend to record the speed of march of armies only
when they are exceptional. Usually these are very fast. In 329 BC
Alexander, with a specially selected 'flying column', covered
about 185 miles in three days (Arrian, *Anabasis* 4.6.4). Sometimes
figures are given because the march was so slow. A Roman army
campaigning in Asia Minor in 189 BC was so laden with booty that it

made a bare six miles in a day's march (Livy 38.15.15). There are so many potential variables – the state of the roads/paths, the weather, the composition of the force, the size and type of the baggage train, the time taken setting up a camp, the proximity of the enemy, and the perceived need for haste – that attempts to produce average figures are difficult. Archaeology can help with some campaigns. Although it is notoriously hard to date Roman marching camps, two groups in northeast Scotland have been identified as belonging to the campaigns of Agricola, in the late 1st century AD, and Septimius Severus, in the early 3rd century AD. The distances between these camps indicate a slow rate of march, less than 15 miles a day.

Campaigns and logistics: 'unhorsing the Huns'

The explanatory possibilities and pitfalls of logistical analyses of ancient armies can be illustrated by taking R. P. Lindner's article 'Nomadism, horses and Huns' as a case study. This work's stated aim is to 'unhorse most of the Huns'. Its conclusion is that when the Huns settled on the Great Hungarian Plain (AD c. 410/420–c. 465) they ceased to be nomads, and thus ceased to fight as cavalry. Two lines of argument are deployed to support these findings: one textual and one ecological. Lindner points out that some contemporary sources do not explicitly refer to the Huns as cavalry, while others that do are dismissed as unhistorical because they follow an earlier description (that of Ammianus Marcellinus 31.2, written AD c. 395). On the ecological line Lindner estimates that the pasturage of the Great Hungarian Plain could feed only about 150,000 grazing nomad horses. By analogy with the later Mongols, it is considered that each Hun needed ten horses, and thus there could have been only 15,000 Hun cavalry in this period.

Some scholars in passing have agreed or disagreed with Lindner, but, as far as I am aware, to date there has been no extended academic engagement with his views. A few comments can be made here.

Literary arguments from silence are always suspect. It could be that some contemporaries did not explicitly describe the Huns as cavalry precisely because everyone knew that they were. To dismiss those sources that do portray the Huns as cavalry as unhistorical because they are indebted to Ammianus might be to read them in an anachronistic way. In classical literary culture it was good to show one's wide reading. As such, it was always apposite to allude to earlier distinguished writers. To give an example, after Thucydides had written a famous description of the plague in Athens in 430 BC (2.47–55), subsequent authors who did plague scenes tended to draw on Thucydides. Which is not to say that the plagues they depicted were imaginary. Ammianus' description of the Huns may have come to occupy a similar position. Furthermore, Lindner makes no mention of some contemporary literary evidence, uninfluenced by Ammianus, which does talk of the Huns as cavalry. Vegetius, whom Lindner takes to be writing in the mid-5th century AD, in his *Epitoma rei militaris*, twice holds up the Huns as model cavalrymen (1.20; 3.26). Also it can be noted that in the next century the Huns who served as mercenaries in the Byzantine army of Belisarius are 'all mounted bowmen' (Procopius 3.11.12).

Even if Lindner's estimates for the grazing potential of the Great Hungarian Plain are correct, problems remain with his deductions. Firstly, Hun society now was very different from its earlier form on the Steppes to the northeast of the Black Sea. The Huns had acquired an autocratic monarchy, social stratification, a huge empire, and, as literary sources show them living in villages, they had indeed ceased to be 'pure' nomads. The Huns were equally adept at extracting agricultural produce from their subjects and tribute from the eastern Roman empire. These could supplement the forage of the Plain, if the Huns were prepared for another change, feeding their horses partly by grain. Secondly, Lindner's analogy with the Mongols is arbitrary. Other figures can be played with. As Lindner states, three changes of horse a day might wear them out. But if the Huns were prepared to risk this, then on the given figures the Plain could have supported 50,000 cavalrymen.

Finally, there is a problem with the idea that if the Huns stopped being nomads then they stopped being cavalry. All Steppe nomads were cavalry, but not all cavalry were nomadic.

After a defeat in Gaul in AD 451 we are told (Jordanes, *Getica* 41.215) that Attila contemplated suicide by burning himself to death on a pyre of his followers' saddles. Lindner comments that this 'is proof not that he had many horsemen but that he led too few'. This may be true in the sense that by this time a large proportion of Attila's army was made up of subject peoples, many of whom fought as infantry. Yet it takes quite a leap of faith to see this as evidence for most of the Huns having given up their horses.

Chapter 6
Fighting

John Keegan's book *The Face of Battle: A Study of Agincourt, Waterloo and the Somme*, published in 1976, popularized a new genre of modern writing about fighting. To the existing type of study which looked at battle from the perspective of the general was added another which looked at the physical and emotional experiences of the ordinary combatant. This chapter follows the latter model, looking in turn at ancient land battle, siege warfare, and naval warfare. In each section a very brief sketch of the development of techniques precedes an exploration of a specific dimension of the psychology of combat. In the final section, we look in detail at one battle; this brings together many of the themes of this book, and acts as a way into an investigation of leadership in classical war.

The hoplite

Consider a Greek hoplite (Figure 9). This one is a bronze statuette dedicated in the sanctuary of Zeus at Dodona in c. 500 BC. The amount of armour worn by a hoplite varied over time. But, with two exceptions, as we will see, this one seems typical. First, let us think about his equipment and its implications for fighting. He wears a bronze helmet, bronze body armour, and greaves. He carries a large shield. This hoplite carries a 'Boeotian' shield, which, like the 'Dipylon' shield we met in Chapter 3, may not have existed in reality.

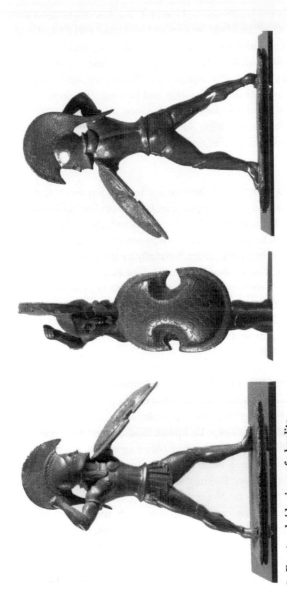

9. Front and side views of a hoplite

Normally the hoplite carried a round, wooden shield faced with bronze, which was held by a central arm band and a hand grip at the edge. The statuette originally held a long thrusting spear in its right hand. Most hoplites would have had a sword as a secondary weapon. The equipment is heavy, hot, and tiring. The helmet cuts down his vision and hearing. He carries nothing with which to fight at a distance. His battle will contain little manoeuvre (how well can he hear or see signals?), be fought hand to hand, and be short (before exhaustion sets in).

Now let us think about the man inside the equipment. Unless he is a Spartan or a mercenary, he is not a professional soldier. Until the Peloponnesian War (431–404 BC), and quite often afterwards, he provides his own equipment, and serves without pay. He is relatively wealthy. Normally he is a farmer. He can be any age from late teens to about sixty. Professional instructors in weapon handling were known by the late 5th century BC, but were always the exception. Dancing and athletics were considered suitable training for combat. The man interacts with his equipment. His battle will be short, simple, and at close quarters.

Finally, let us imagine this individual's place in the battle as a whole, using the most commonly accepted interpretation of hoplite combat. He takes his place in a phalanx: a closely packed body of men several ranks deep. He knows those around him, probably some of them are related to him. After an animal has been sacrificed, and the general has made a speech, the phalanx sets off towards the enemy. The men move at a walk, and sing the *paean*, or hymn, of their *polis*. Nearing the enemy, they break into a run, and shout a simple war cry. The aim is to crash into contact with the enemy. If their opponents are another phalanx, the *othismos*, or push, may result. This has been compared to a huge rugby scrum with deadly weapons added. The rear ranks physically push on the backs of those in front. Sooner or later one side will establish a forward momentum, and the losing side will break and run. Many casualties occur. Estimates put average casualties at about 5 per cent for the winners, and 14 per cent for the losers.

Some scholars see hoplite battle in a different way. They interpret the *othismos* as a figure of speech, arguing either that the rear ranks provided just moral support, or that hoplites actually fought in a looser formation altogether. It could be that a search for the norm is doomed to failure. Just as different Greek states adopted the hoplite phalanx at different times, so they may have developed somewhat different styles. We know that Spartans walked into contact, and that Thebans tended to fight in deeper formations than was the norm. It could be that the phalanx of a *polis* further varied its practice according to the circumstances of the day.

The hoplite phalanx was dominant in Greek pitched battle through the 7th to the later 4th centuries BC. Other troop types, light infantry and cavalry, were not unknown, and their use increased from the Peloponnesian War onwards. Yet there was a tendency to marginalize them, both in reality on the battlefield and ideologically by those writing history, because of the social and political control exercised by the hoplite class in most Greek states.

The phalangite

The armies with which Philip II of Macedon achieved hegemony over Greece, his son Alexander conquered the Persian empire, and the latter's successors and the Hellenistic kingdoms they founded dominated the eastern Mediterranean were forces of combined arms. They consisted of a phalanx of heavy infantry for close combat, light infantry, and cavalry. The light infantry were equipped with javelins, slings, or bows, and operated as was conventional throughout antiquity, attempting to harass from a distance the main body of the enemy, while protecting the rest of their own side. The distinctive Macedonian cavalry were shock troops, although units of other cavalry made contributions (we will look at how cavalry functioned later on in this chapter). The core of a Macedonian-style army were the men in the phalanx. We know less about these phalangites than some modern works might lead one to assume. Our sources, literary and artistic, for Macedonian war-making tend to be about Alexander, and to focus closely on the figure of the king. As in pitched battle Alexander fought with the cavalry, we are poorly informed about the infantry. Our best source on the Macedonian phalanx, Polybius (18.28–32), was writing, in the second half of the 2nd century BC, to explain how the phalanx had been defeated by the Roman legions. Although Macedonian battle had changed, the phalanx becoming the main battle winner as the numbers and shock capacity of cavalry declined, Polybius seems to overstate his case that the phalanx was inflexible and incapable of operating in broken ground. Earlier, Alexander's phalanx at the battle of Issus (333 BC), although it was roughly handled by an opposing phalanx of mercenary Greek hoplites, had been able to alter its depth and frontage on the battlefield and to fight across a river. As late as 197 BC, at the battle of Cynoscephalae, one wing of the Macedonian phalanx operating on a hillside was driving its Roman opponents back until attacked from behind.

The Macedonian phalanx's key difference from a hoplite phalanx was its main weapon, the *sarissa*. Much scholarly effort has been devoted to the *sarissa*, with no end in sight. At least all agree that it was a long pike that was wielded with both hands. Its length allowed the spear-points of the first four or five ranks of the phalanx to project beyond the foremost men, as opposed to the two or three of a hoplite phalanx. The idea appears to have been to increase the width of the killing zone and the number of sharp points within it. The aim was to present the enemy with an impenetrable barrier of spear-points some feet from the phalanx itself. We should not elevate the *sarissa* to the status of a 'superweapon'. If it had been, it is unlikely that the Spartans would have waited for over a hundred years after its appearance on Greek battlefields before introducing it into their own armies in 227 BC. For most Macedonian phalangites, as for most Greek hoplites, the battlefield must have been a place of very limited knowledge. Only the first few ranks could have any view of what was going on. The majority – tightly packed in the body of the phalanx, their view obscured by their colleagues and the dust kicked up, and their hearing assaulted by the din – would have been unable to form any objective understanding of the course of the battle. This being so, the morale of the phalangites was especially susceptible to noises which suggested that they were in danger to the flanks or rear, or any impression that the phalanx was giving ground.

The legionary

It seems that the Romans, like their neighbours the Etruscans, adopted the hoplite phalanx, probably at some point in the 7th or 6th centuries BC. In the 4th century BC, however, they seem to have instituted the famous legion. Over time, the organization of the legion changed, most notably from a formation centred on 30 small sub-units called maniples, as described by Polybius, to one of 10 larger sub-units called cohorts, as found in the writings of Julius Caesar. Similarly, its personnel altered from a militia of Italian farmers to long-service professionals recruited mainly from the provinces under the principate. Yet, apart from the disappearance of the spear, carried by a minority in Polybius' description, the equipment of legionaries remained remarkably the same from our earliest evidence down to the later 3rd century AD. Legionaries wore a metal helmet and, usually, body armour, and carried a large, curved shield (*scutum*), one or two heavy javelins (*pila*, singular *pilum*), a sword (*gladius*), and a dagger (*pugio*).

Our evidence does not allow any certainty to reconstructions of the frontage occupied by a legionary in the battle line. The most common estimates are six or three feet. It is possible that the frontage varied over time or was dependent on the specific circumstances of the battle. Although the legionary could be ordered to use his *pilum* as a thrusting weapon, normally against cavalry, it was primarily a throwing weapon, and its weight gave it only a short range. In Caesar's account of the battle of Pharsalus, we find a debate over the relative merits of momentum and cohesion (*Civil War* 3.92). Was it better to risk a loss of cohesion but gain momentum by charging, or reverse these goals by standing to receive an attack? Caesar and most Roman generals preferred the former.

Against other infantry the legionary would expect to advance into combat, throwing his *pilum* on command as part of a volley. While the shower of *pila* disordered the enemy, the legionary should draw his sword and close to hand to hand combat. The sword could be employed to stab or slash. The shield could be used offensively. Held by a central grip, and furnished with a metal boss, it could be punched into the face of an opponent, or, with the legionary's shoulder behind it, be used to knock the enemy off balance. Comparison of skeletons from Maiden Castle in Britain, which was stormed by the Romans, with the far more numerous ones from the medieval battle of Wisby suggests that the aim of a legionary was to get his opponent on the ground and then butcher him with numerous heavy cuts to the head from his sword (see Figure 14, page 120). That such fighting was physically exhausting – and we can estimate that some infantry battles, like Cannae, lasted for hours – has led some modern scholars to hypothesize that at times such combat reverted to a 'default state', where the two sides would draw back and hurl missiles and insults at each other as they got their courage up for another short burst of hand to hand fighting. In such a 'slogging match', the legionary would be physically helped by his training. We are told that they trained with heavier weapons than those they used in combat (Vegetius 1.11). Also, psychologically he would be aided by both the concept of discipline (*disciplina*), which Romans considered that they had and all other peoples lacked, and the warrior myths of Rome which stressed the 'long haul', such as the mythical Horatio holding the bridge against an overwhelming force.

The cavalry

As Greece consists of a collection of arid and rugged peninsulas and islands, it is unsurprising that, although the ownership of horses was a mark of elite status, cavalry was not the main striking force of classical Greek armies, with the exception of those from the broader plains of Thessaly in the north. Still further north, the wide pastures and tribal society of Macedonia allowed the development of the effective cavalry which formed a vital element in the armies with which Philip II subdued Greece and Alexander conquered the Persian empire and various Indian peoples as far as the River Indus. Under the Hellenistic kingdoms which succeeded Alexander, the numbers and effectiveness of cavalry declined. Under the Republic, the Romans appear to have had a small but effective body of citizen cavalry. This, however, disappeared in the early 1st century BC, and, although very small numbers of citizen cavalry reappeared in the principate, Roman armies henceforth relied on foreign or subject auxiliary cavalry. From earliest times, cavalry was of secondary importance to heavy infantry in Roman armies. This began to change in the second half of the 3rd century AD. Roman armies of the 4th and 5th centuries relied heavily on cavalry, and by the 6th and 7th centuries, although infantry remained numerically dominant, the cavalry were the main strike force of the empire's armies.

The types of cavalry in the ancient world can be imagined as a spectrum. At one end were true light cavalry, such as the Numidian and Moorish horsemen of North Africa. These relied on missile weapons and tried to avoid hand to hand combat altogether, or at least until the enemy were running. They used the speed and manoeuvrability of their horses to make themselves into mobile missile platforms. At the other end of the spectrum were true 'shock' cavalry, such as Alexander's Companion cavalry. These were equipped only for close combat. As horses cannot be made to run into solid objects that they are unable to see through or jump, such as close-packed bodies of infantry, 'shock' cavalry rely on the combined bulk of horse and man to intimidate their opponents into running, or at least breaking the frontage of their formation so that the cavalrymen can get amongst them and ride or cut them down as individuals.

The potential of ancient cavalry can be illustrated by thinking about Plutarch's account of the first, decisive day of the battle of Carrhae in 53 BC (*Crassus* 23–27). A Parthian army comprised entirely of cavalry, the majority light horse archers, with a smaller number of armoured cavalry equipped with lances, confronted a much larger Roman army, of legionaries supported by light infantry and cavalry, commanded by Crassus. A first charge by the Parthian cavalry was not pressed home as the legionaries presented a dense, unbroken line. This formation, however, gave the Parthian light archers an ideal target. The Romans endured the missiles believing that the Parthians would run out of ammunition. When it was seen that the horse archers were being resupplied, Crassus ordered his son, Publius, to attack with the right wing of the army. The Parthians retreated, shooting as they went, until Publius' troops were separated from the main body. The Parthians then placed a unit of heavy cavalry to the front of Publius' men. Publius was unable to persuade his infantry to attack, and so was bested in a cavalry melee. Falling back on his infantry, Publius drew up his remaining men on a small hill. There they were shot down by the Parthians, before finally being overrun by the heavy cavalry. The Parthians then turned back to the main body of Roman troops, the heavy cavalry attacking the front with their long lances, while the bowmen poured arrows into the flanks. When nightfall halted the battle, the Roman army had ceased to be an effective fighting force.

Motivation: only a few fight?

John Keegan's *The Face of Battle* has encouraged classical historians to apply the conclusions of studies of psychology in modern combat to the ancient world. One example can illustrate the methodological care that must be employed in such work. In *Men Against Fire*, published in 1947, S. L. A. Marshall claimed that among American troops at the sharp end in the Second World War only one in four ever fired their weapon. A. K. Goldsworthy has applied this to the Roman army in two ways. Finding it implausible that men in close formations could have taken no action, he suggested that 75 per cent of missile troops took no aim when shooting, and the same percentage of heavy infantry would fight only defensively at close quarters. This straightforward transference must be doubted. Marshall himself did not think his figures were a universal norm. In a later work he argued that those firing had gone up to between 37 per cent and 55 per cent in the Korean War. Historians of modern war are now suspicious of Marshall's statistics. Yet even were they correct, there are reasons to doubt their applicability to the ancient world.

Three steps should be taken when investigating whether a concept from modern military studies of combat motivation can be applied to the classical world: can any support be found in the ancient evidence; were the physical environments of battle close enough to allow the concept to 'work' in the ancient world; and did the underlying factors causing the phenomenon in modern times also exist in the past? On all three counts, the idea that only one in four Romans fought aggressively fails. We can use as a case study the anonymous *War in Spain* (*Bellum Hispaniense*) preserved among the works of Julius Caesar. This understudied, brief continuation of Caesar's *Commentaries* gives us a rare view from someone below the higher ranks of society. Uninformed on the larger issues of strategy, the author is interested in the weather, soldier's pay, low-level desertions, and military punishments. Long ago, Lord Macaulay guessed that he was 'some sturdy centurion, who fought better than he wrote'. While the author does think that soldiers had different feelings waiting for battle to commence, and that the inexperienced on the other side were numbed with fear by the noise of combat, when he describes fighting, the men in units act as one. They all shoot, fight hand to hand, and refuse to close to combat, give ground, or run away. The only two exceptions do not fit the 'one in four' model are two individuals fighting a duel, and two centurions making the ultimate, individual sacrifice in an attempt to put heart in all the rest of the unit. The physical circumstances of American GIs and Roman troops were very different. The former tended to be prone and relatively isolated. The latter usually were standing and surrounded by comrades. Finally, apart from fear, Marshall thought that it was the Christian commandment 'Thou shalt not kill' that froze the GI's trigger finger. It should go without saying that until the 4th century AD, and quite often after then, Roman soldiers were not Christians. Roman society was violent, with a legal right, even a moral imperative, to violent self-defence. Public executions drew big crowds, and gladiators were sex symbols. Although 'Thou shalt not kill' really was not an issue for a legionary, raising the question of the applicability of Marshall's idea to the ancient world was not a waste of time. We learn something about both when we see the ancient world as being different from ours.

Siege warfare

Epic sieges were prominent in the classical civilizations' views of their early history: for the Greeks the ten-year siege of Troy, and for the Romans the siege of Veii, suspiciously also thought to have lasted ten years. Despite this, Greece and Rome lagged behind the Near East in the development of siege warfare. The Persians, who invaded Greece in 480 BC, were equipped with all the techniques of siegecraft known to the ancient world, except one. That was torsion-powered artillery, which with stones as projectiles was used against walls, and with stones or bolts against personnel. The invention of this artillery is to be placed at the court of either Dionysius I the tyrant of Syracuse (405–367 BC) or Philip II of Macedon (359–336 BC). The Romans refined existing techniques, and from the principate onwards enjoyed an advantage in siege warfare over all contemporary peoples, except the Sassanid Persians.

Writing a good set piece description of a siege was one of the marks of a good historian in the ancient world. Among literary depictions, particularly important are Thucydides on Plataea (431–427 BC), Diodorus Siculus on Rhodes (305–304 BC), Julius Caesar on Alesia (52 BC), Josephus on Jerusalem (AD 70), and Ammianus Marcellinus on Amida (AD 359). From these and archaeological evidence (particularly important sites are Dura-Europos on the Euphrates and Masada in Israel), we can build up a composite picture of a siege.

To take a walled town or fortress, the attackers had to get through, over, or under its defences. Mining was employed for the latter. Subterranean tunnels were dug which could have two aims: to enable troops to emerge behind the defences, or to create a breach by undermining them. Other ways to create a breach were for the base of the walls to be weakened by sappers with pickaxes and crowbars, by battering rams, or, if available, by stone-throwing artillery. To get over the walls called for scaling ladders, movable siege towers, or earth and wood ramps. The attackers would use what missile troops and artillery they possessed to try to prevent the enemy interfering with their operations.

The defenders were seldom inactive. They might dig their own mines, either seeking to undermine a ramp, or to break into and collapse the attackers' mine. The entombed bodies of Roman and Sassanid Persian soldiers at Dura-Europos provide eloquent testimony to the horrors of such underground fighting. Hooks or chains might be used to try to 'catch', and thus render ineffective, a battering ram, or 'padding' might be lowered in front of the wall to absorb the impact of rams or projectiles. A second, or even third, wall might be built behind where a breach threatened. The defenders would use whatever projectiles they could to hinder the attackers' efforts. At any point the defenders might sally out from their walls to try to cause havoc among the besieging force.

Ancient stories of the wonderful, and often implausible, inventions of Archimedes defending Syracuse from the Romans (213–211 BC) show that siege warfare was at the cutting edge of ancient technology. Despite this, many defended places fell to surprise, trickery, treachery, or were starved into surrender.

Sieges were very expensive, and called for high logistic sophistication. They often lasted for a long time, during which troops usually had to be paid, and they demanded huge amounts of supplies: food and fodder for the besieging force, as well as the raw materials to construct siege works. Often these materials would have to be transported long distances. Not all supplies and transport could be requisitioned; some would have to be paid for. The siege of Potidaea (432–430 BC) absorbed two-fifths of the reserves of Athens at the height of its prosperity. Conversely, a successful siege could yield enormous amounts of booty, including slaves.

The normal rules of war did not apply in siege warfare. Various explanations can be offered of why siege fighting was so much bloodier than most land battles. One is the lack of control experienced by ancient commanders when their troops were scattered in built-up areas. Another seeks to invoke biological theories: the so-called 'flight or fight' mechanism released when too many aggressive humans or rats are placed in too confined a space. A third argues that the troops were attempting to reassert their control of battle, which had been subverted by engineers during the siege. Another explanation can be offered. Ancient land battles were over quickly, within a day, or at most two or three. Sieges could last for weeks, months, or even years. Throughout this time, the besiegers were in constant danger, both from sallies by the enemy, and from the clearly recognized threat of disease. The extremes of brutality employed in sacking a city may have stemmed from desires for 'revenge' on an enemy which was thought of as having placed the attacking troops in an extended position of fear.

Naval warfare

Consider a Greek warship (see Figure 10). This is the *Olympias*, a modern reconstruction of an Athenian *trireme*. The *Olympias* is a triumph of experimental archaeology, drawing on a wide variety of different disciplines, including recent developments in underwater archaeology. Yet the ship can never tell us the full potential of a *trireme*. The modern crews have different physiques from ancient ones, and lack the latter's inherited skills. No one will suggest that *Olympias* be tested to destruction. It is not part of the project to see how nastily the crew of a *trireme* can drown.

Although *triremes* used sails, as in the picture, they were not the main form of propulsion, and were usually left ashore before a battle. A *trireme* was a galley with a ram, rowed by 170 men arranged in three banks. There were two approaches to fighting with *triremes*. The 'light' school centralized skilled manoeuvre, and sought to use the ram either to hole and waterlog the enemy, or to render them immobile by sheering away the oars on one side of their vessel. The distinctive tactics of the 'light' school were the *periplous*, an outflanking manoeuvre, and the *diekplous*, an attempt to break through the enemy line of battle. The 'heavy' school sometimes reinforced the prows of their *triremes* and attempted ram-to-ram collisions, but more normally relied on grappling and boarding. If threatened by a fleet of superior skill, the *kyklos*, a close circle with rams pointing out, might be adopted.

The earliest literary mention of a *trireme* dates to the mid-6th century BC. From then to the late 4th century BC, *triremes* were the standard battleship in the Mediterranean. After which time heavier warships, concentrating on boarding over manoeuvre, dominated. These had numerical names, such as 'fours', 'fives', and so on. It is most probable that they were still rowed on three levels, but with more than one rower at all or some of the oars. The Roman and

10. A reconstruction of the trireme *Olympias*

Carthaginian fleets of the Punic Wars were built around 'fives' (*Quinqueremes*), and Roman fleets in the civil wars of the last century BC tended to employ yet bigger ships. Under the principate, with the absence of any credible naval threat, Roman fleets were largely composed of smaller vessels, including *triremes*. We last hear of *triremes* in action in a Roman civil war in AD 323 (Zosimus 2.22.2; 2.23.3–4). By the 5th century, we are told that the techniques of building *triremes* have been forgotten (Zosimus 5.20.3–4). When in the 6th century AD the Byzantine empire again began to build large naval forces, their standard warship, the *dromon*, was of different design from classical galleys.

The limited strategic outreach of ancient warships in part was due to their relatively poor seaworthiness, and in part to their lack of storage space. Although ancient warships could take on supplies for some days, it was normal for them to beach both at midday to take on water and for the crew to eat, and overnight for the crew to sleep ashore as well. Unlike naval sailing vessels of the 18th and 19th centuries, ancient warships could not operate for long independent of the land, and thus could not enforce a blockade on a distant shore.

Naval warfare, like siege warfare, called for vast resources and employed the most advanced technology of the ancient world, and thus it was very expensive. During the Peloponnesian War, Athens lost two large fleets in a disastrous expedition to Sicily (415–413 BC). By a supreme financial effort, Athens built a replacement battle fleet. But when this fleet was lost at Aegospotami (405 BC) Athens could not afford to rebuild again and the war was over. Their Spartan opponents were in a different position. In return for renouncing (however falsely) any intentions of liberating the Greeks of Asia Minor, the Spartans began to receive Persian financial aid (412/411 BC). The Spartans thus could suffer repeated large defeats at sea, such as Cyzicus (410 BC) and Arginusae (406 BC), yet still continue the war, as they could afford to replace the ships and men they lost.

The high costs of a fleet can be illustrated by thinking about the Athenian institution of the *Trierarchy*. This was a sort of wealth tax to pay for the running of warships. In theory, while Athens provided the hull, rigging, and pay and provisions for a *trireme*, a rich Athenian individual was appointed as *Trierarch* to act as captain and pay for repairs. In practice, Athens provided the pay and provisions retrospectively, only half being up front in the 5th century BC, and nothing in the 4th. Also *Trierarchs*, for their own glory and both physical and financial security (as they both served on the ship and would be responsible for its loss), tended to buy their own rigging and to hire skilled crews out of their own pocket. As the financial position of Athens deteriorated, it became harder to find enough individuals to be *Trierarchs*. During the Peloponnesian War, two men (*Syntrierarchs*) were appointed to share a *Trierarchy*, and in the 350s BC the 1,200 richest men in Athens were organized in 20 groups (*Symmoriai*) to bear the total *trierarchic* costs.

The financial costs of serving as a *Trierarch* are illuminated wonderfully by a speech from the 4th century BC preserved among the works of Demosthenes (*Or.* 50), although not composed by him. This speech was written for (and possibly by) the Athenian banker Apollodorus. As a rich man and as a new citizen wishing to make his mark, Apollodorus had lavishly equipped his *trireme*. Apollodorus' patriotism was abused. Apollodorus' *trireme*, as one of the best equipped, was sent by his commander on extra missions. These included a trip back to Piraeus, the port of Athens, where Apollodorus' crew demanded more money to re-embark. In the speech Apollodorus is suing for the additional expenses incurred because his successor avoided taking over the ship for over five months. Evocative as this speech is, when reading it we should not take it as unbiased reportage, but remember that it is a forensic oration designed to persuade a jury.

It is striking that in ancient naval battle morale tended to operate at the level not of the individual rowers but the ship. As an example we can take Thucydides' account of the Spartan defeat at Naupactus in 430 BC.

> the deck-hands were shouting and taking evasive action, and abusing one another, so that they were not listening for the words of command or for the boatswains, and as the ill-trained oarsmen, being unable to clear their oars in the choppy water, made the ships unresponsive to the helm, at that precise moment . . . the Athenians moved in to ram. In the confusion none of the Spartan ships fought, but all fled.
>
> (*Thucydides* 2.84, slightly abridged)

For the Spartan ships to flee, their rowers, despite being ill-trained and in physical difficulties, had not given way to individual panic, but were still operating as a team. The collapse in morale rested with the *Trierarchs*. We can suggest why that might have been by considering some comparative history. In an enthralling study of the British navy of the 18th century, N. A. M. Rodger found that in battle, while some individual sailors might attempt to leave their posts and hide in the hold out of immediate harm's way, the vast majority, having a limited appreciation of the overall course of the combat, were kept too busy to give way to fear. The opposite was the case for the ships' commanders. They had a good view of wider events, were in an exposed position, and, not being called on to perform continuous physical activity, had plenty of time to dwell on the risks that they were running, and decide that enough was enough. We can imagine that much the same applied to the commanders and crew of ancient warships. For the latter, there was not even a hold in which to try to hide.

Winter quarters: exploring a battle and leadership

A shortage of grain throughout Gaul, caused by a drought the previous summer (54 BC), led Julius Caesar to break from his normal practice and divide his army when it went into winter quarters. At Atuatuca, somewhere in the Ardennes, one division, comprised of a legion recently raised in northern Italy, another five cohorts (equivalent to half a legion), and some Spanish auxiliary cavalry, were snug in thatched wooden huts, well supplied with provisions, and protected by a ditch and rampart sited in a strong position. The local tribe, the Eburones, seemed docile. Their leaders, Ambiorix and Catuvolcus, had met the Romans at their borders, and had brought corn into the cantonment. After about 15 days, all appeared peaceful. A detachment of the troops was out gathering wood, and the rest were unarmed in the camp, when the attack came. The detachment was overrun. In the camp the legionaries ran to arm themselves, and, taking their places on the rampart, tried to fight off the assault. When the Spanish horses sallied out and got the advantage of the Gallic cavalry, the tribesmen drew back.

The Eburones asked for a parley. Ambiorix, through Roman intermediaries, offered on oath a safe conduct to the besieged force. The Gallic chief said that it had not been his wish to attack. His hand had been forced by his own people, who had been encouraged to act by a general rising throughout Gaul; all Caesar's camps were under attack, and a large force of Germans had crossed the Rhine and would be at Atuatuca in two days. At the officers' council of war held on receipt of this message, a deep division emerged between the two Roman commanders. Cotta argued that they should stay put. Sabinus, raising his voice so that the soldiers could hear, demanded that they should go. At midnight Cotta yielded, and it was announced that they would march at dawn. The soldiers passed the rest of the night talking and going through their possessions to decide what they would abandon in the camp.

At first light it was a straggling column of tired soldiers impeded by much baggage that marched out into the heavily wooded landscape. After about two miles the column entered a steep defile. As the vanguard tried to climb the ascent out, the ambush was sprung. Ambiorix had lied. There was no general revolt in Gaul, and no

Germans rushing to aid it. He had led his tribe into the attack, and he had no intention of keeping to the safe conduct. The noise in the Roman camp had given the Eburones warning that the Romans would march that morning.

With the army assailed from all sides, the Roman generals reacted very differently. Sabinus ran about issuing ineffectual orders to post the cohorts here and there. Cotta, however, addressed the troops to encourage them, and fought like a soldier. As the length of the column made effective supervision impossible, the generals ordered their men to form a square. This manoeuvre, smacking of despair, merely encouraged the enemy, and lowered Roman morale. In a confusion of shouting and weeping, Roman soldiers were abandoning their posts in attempts to retrieve their treasured possessions from the baggage train. The Eburones obeyed their leaders and kept in rank, rather than attempting to loot the Roman baggage. Seeing that the Romans were still causing many casualties in hand-to-hand combat, Ambiorix ordered his men to fight with missiles from a distance. The cohorts that charged could not catch the Gauls, whose mobility was enhanced by the lightness of their equipment and their daily training. The charging Romans were pelted with missiles on their unshielded right side, and when they attempted to retire were surrounded and cut down. For nearly eight hours those who remained close-packed in the square endured a rain of missiles. In response to a request from Sabinus, Ambiorix said that if the general wished for a parley he would guarantee his life and would try to prevail on the tribesmen to spare the rest of the Romans. Cotta, who had been wounded in the face by a slingshot, refused to negotiate with an enemy under arms. Sabinus ordered those officers nearby to accompany him. Commanding the Roman party to cast away their arms, Ambiorix span out the negotiations until they were surrounded and killed. On the death of Sabinus, the barbarians, raising their customary shouts, charged back into close-quarter combat. Cotta died fighting.

Some of the Romans managed to fight their way back to their camp.

The legionary eagle was saved by the self-sacrifice of the standard-bearer, and the remnant held out until nightfall. Realizing that their position was hopeless, that night they slew one another to the last man. Out of the whole army only a handful survived, slipping away through the woods.

We are well informed about the disaster at Atuatuca in the winter of 54–53 BC. Several ancient sources tell of it. Yet all are derived from one text: Julius Caesar's *Commentaries* (*Gallic War* 5.24–37). These can be described as propaganda, in the sense that Caesar seeks to convince a Roman readership of the rightness and the greatness of his actions. We cannot be sure how many legionaries, and thus Roman citizens, plus auxiliaries, died at Atuatuca. A legion at this time probably contained about 5,000 men. The main legion in this force was recently raised, so probably had not had time to reach the levels of undermanning which seem to have been common. On any estimate thousands of citizens under the ultimate command of Caesar had been massacred. Caesar had some explaining to do, and it is fascinating to see how he seeks to free himself of blame.

First, he is at pains to show how accurate is his account; he knows about the event from both sides. The few Romans who got away escaped to the camp of another deputy, Labienus, who sent Caesar a letter telling their story. Later, when Caesar captured some of the Eburones, he learned more details, and he lets us know that he has subsequently been to Atuatuca. Second, Caesar attempts to show that he had taken every possible precaution. The need for supplies had forced him to divide his army. Yet he had made sure that all the winter quarters were at no great distance from one another, and he was waiting in Gaul until he heard that all the camps were fortified and supplied. Third, Caesar shifts almost all the blame on to Sabinus (we will look below at how Caesar portrays the actions of the soldiers). The behaviour of Sabinus is marked by stupidity; if it was foolish to trust a Gaul once, it was doubly so to trust him a second time after he had broken his oath. In council Sabinus betrays signs of demagoguery in raising his voice so that the ordinary soldiers can hear him. He panics when they are ambushed. There is even a suggestion of duplicitous cowardice; asking Cotta to join him in negotiating with Ambiorix, Sabinus suppresses the fact that the Gaul has already promised to spare Sabinus' life, but not those of the other Romans. Later in the text (5.52), Caesar tells his troops not to be downhearted because of this disaster, it was entirely the fault of Sabinus and his *temeritas* (rashness or perfidy). Sabinus' dreadful performance is made evident in the text as Caesar goes on to write up at length (5.39–52) the excellent behaviour of Quintus Cicero (the famous orator's brother) under almost identical circumstances: when his camp is attacked he turns down the overtures of the Gauls and conducts a vigorous defence until rescued by Caesar.

Apart from the drought of 54 BC being evident in the tree-ring record, archaeology provides no direct evidence for the battle. Atuatuca is often identified as Tongres in Belgium, but the scanty and imprecise topographical details furnished by Caesar allow no certainty. It was in Caesar's interests to emphasize the natural strength of the site of the winter quarters, and the Ardennes are full of wooded defiles. In contrast, the site of a similar disaster of even greater magnitude which befell a Roman force under Varus in AD 9 in the Teutoburg Forest in Germany, outside the modern town of Kalkriese, has recently yielded a mass of evidence. Among the many items of Roman equipment found, one is especially poignant; the skeleton of a baggage mule, the large bronze bell around its neck stuffed with straw in an attempt to deaden its sound and not give away the movements of the army. If we consider what archaeologists call the formation of an archaeological site (in this case, broadly what has happened to the site between the event and its discovery/excavation), the contrasting fate of the two battlefields in the archaeological record becomes clear. Although a later Roman expedition reached the site of Varus' defeat and buried some of the bodies, the battlefield remained outside the empire in the territory of free German tribes. It seems that the Germans left the bodies of the Romans and some of their equipment on the battlefield as a dedication to the gods. For the Germans, the site became a sacred, lasting memorial to their triumph. The aftermath was very different at Atuatuca. The Romans recaptured the area within weeks, and for centuries it remained within the province of Gallia Belgica. The Romans had reasons beyond piety for burying their dead and tidying up the battlefield.

The events at Atuatuca forcibly remind us of the importance of logistics in ancient strategy and tactics. The need to find supplies forced Caesar to divide his army, and the overlong baggage train contributed to Sabinus' defeat. The beating back of two Gallic assaults on the camp at Atuatuca and Quintus Cicero's successful defence of his camp under days of continuous attack by huge numbers of barbarians point to the superiority in siege warfare enjoyed from the 4th century BC onwards by the Greeks and Romans over almost all other contemporary cultures. One of the very few meaningful constants over centuries of warfare appears to be the ability of well-supplied regular troops in fortifications to defy seemingly overwhelming numbers of irregular warriors. Atuatuca shows the potential of terrain in ancient battle. On steep, wooded slopes the heavily armed Romans could not catch the more lightly equipped Gauls, who were accustomed to those conditions. Deployment on the small area of open, flat ground at the bottom of the defile packed the Romans so close together that they could not fight effectively and made them an easy target for missiles. Although equipment matters, in Caesar's account it is morale that determines success or failure. He indicates fatigue as an important factor in undermining the will to combat. We are told that the Gauls were the equals of the Romans in courage (*virtus*), and it is the effect on the morale of both sides of the death of Sabinus and the officers with him that is the turning point. This testifies to the relatively 'low-technology' nature of ancient land battle.

That the last Romans choose mass suicide rather than try to surrender makes manifest the barbaric nature of their opponents. This is a clash of cultures between those who fight in the 'Western

Way of War' and those who do not. Much in Caesar's account of the Gauls in this battle fits the conventional template of the barbarian. They lie and, being irreligious, break their oaths. In battle they are noisy and prefer ambush and long-distance combat to open, hand-to-hand fighting. Yet Caesar also plays with his audience's expectations. Although he stresses the collective courage of the Romans and gives us vignettes of individual heroism, here and there they behave rather like barbarians. The legionaries lack discipline, first when they chatter all night, tiring themselves and alerting the enemy, and second when, shouting and weeping, they desert their posts in battle to rescue their personal possessions. Conversely, the barbarians at times behave almost like Romans. They have been training daily, obey orders, and keep in their ranks rather than individually loot the Roman baggage. Caesar's partial inversion of classical cultural expectations is made more acceptable to his audience by the information that the main Roman legion is composed of raw recruits; it implies that they had not yet achieved Roman *disciplina*. Yet in his final analysis, blame lay not with the troops but with their commander Sabinus.

One of the most striking features of Caesar's account of Atuatuca is his judgement of the actions of the two Roman generals. Sabinus, the general of whom he disapproves, 'ran to and fro arranging the cohorts; but even this he did nervously and in a way which showed that he was at his wits' end – as generally happens to those who are compelled to make decisions when a battle has actually begun'. While Cotta, the general who is held to have taken the correct course, 'did everything possible to save the army – calling upon the men and encouraging them as their commander-in-chief [Caesar himself] might have done, and fighting in the ranks like a soldier' (5.33, tr. H. J. Edwards). A modern reader might consider that if one's army was caught in an ambush while out of formation in a straggling column, trying to achieve some tactical order was as important as words of encouragement and adding one man to the fighting line, if not rather more so. But that is not Caesar's judgement. This reminds us that, contrary to much that has been written on the subject, generalship is not a universally constant activity. What generals do, and are expected to do, in battle are products of their culture.

In Homer's *Iliad* the leaders are heroes. They can make tactical decisions both before and during battle. Nestor gives his fellow Greek leaders advice on the drawing up of the battle line (2.362–8), and is described getting his own men in order (4.293–309). In combat Hector organizes the Trojans into five units to attack the enemy camp (12.81–7). Yet these are exceptional passages in a long poem. Usually the heroes, who are to be understood as being continuously accompanied by a personal retinue, move around the battlefield, or even completely away from it, at their discretion. They lead by example, attempting with their words to encourage the fighters on their side and depress the spirits of their foes, while seeking glory in personal combat. They belong to the category of commanders who always fight in battle, although not all through the day.

Less changed than we might have expected with the coming of the hoplite phalanx. The hoplite general was busy just before combat. He would draw up his battle line. He took part in an animal sacrifice to gauge the attitude and/or secure the favour of the gods. We emphatically should not dismiss this as a charade, either because it seems very alien to us, or because in some examples the 'result' was rigged. He made a speech to his troops. The reality of this practice should not be dismissed either on the grounds that the pre-battle speeches we have in literary texts are the composition of the author not the general, or because of the practical difficulties in a general making himself heard by many in a large army. The general gave the signal for the phalanx to advance. The general had been brought up on Homer, and thus the perceived need to encourage the fighters, and the desire to prove himself among the *aristos* (the best) caused him to fight in the front rank. It is commonly believed that this, with the absence of a clear command structure and the troops' lack of training, in all except Spartan armies, served to preclude almost any tactical manoeuvre in hoplite battle during its first incarnation, c. 725–431 BC. The two phalanxes advanced straight towards each other. It seems strange to us that with the change from Homeric to hoplite battle, which could be thought a change from 'primitive' to 'civilized' battle, the symbolic element of the general's role remained constant, while the practical side somewhat declined, as the ability to reorganize troops once combat had been joined lessened.

The period from roughly the Peloponnesian War, 431–404 BC, into the 4th century BC saw an increasing complexity on the Greek battlefield. Hoplites remained the mainstay of Greek *polis* armies, but greater roles were given to cavalry and light infantry, and more sophisticated tactics were attempted. For example, at the battle of Mantinaea in 362 BC the Thebans opened with a charge of combined cavalry and light infantry, then attacked with one wing of their phalanx, while 'refusing' the other. In the 4th century BC literature which explored the theory of military command appeared, with such works as Xenophon's *On the Cavalry Commander* and *The Education of Cyrus*, and ideas were expressed which seemed to undermine the role of the general as a physical combatant. The Athenian general Iphicrates said that he was not a cavalryman, hoplite, archer, or peltast (light infantryman), but someone who knew how to direct all of them (Plutarch, *Sayings of Kings and Commanders* 187B). Yet attempts at manoeuvre after the initial setting out of the battle line remained rare, and prone to confusion and disaster. One reason for the Spartan defeat at the battle of Leuctra in 371 BC was the disruption brought about by trying to change formation by increasing the depth of their phalanx at the moment of contact. An expectation remained that the general would take his place at the front, and many generals seemed to have lived up to it. At Leuctra the great Theban general Epaminondas appears to have been in the front line when during the *othismos*, the 'push', he shouted 'give me one step [forward] and we shall have the victory' (Polyaenus 2.3.3). The hoplite general even in this period seems to have been a commander who usually fought in battle, and if he did probably fought for the duration.

The kings of Macedon were the heirs to both ancient and modern Greek thinking on generalship. Alexander was said to sleep with a copy of the *Iliad* under his pillow, and Philip II had been a hostage in the Thebes of Epaminondas. They were also the inheritors of indigenous Macedonian thinking about warriors. It was a cultural ideal that a Macedonian should not wear the belt of an adult until he had killed a man in battle. Given the confluence of these two types of thinking, it is unsurprising that the kings took their place in the forefront of battle. They endured the consequences. Among many other wounds, Philip II lost an eye, and Alexander suffered a punctured lung. Despite leading from the front, they seem to have been more able than earlier Greek commanders to implement tactical changes during battle. At the battle of Chaeronea in 338 BC Philip II, while standing in the front line (Polyaenus 4.2.2), managed to get his phalanx to make a tactical withdrawal while actually in contact with the enemy (Diodorus 16.86.4). That such manoeuvres were possible was due to three factors. First, the Macedonian army did have an effective chain of command. Second, its troops were sufficiently well trained to put into effect new orders. Third, the kings must have had some respite from physically fighting. Either it was possible for them to temporarily withdraw through the ranks, or, as was suggested above, battle at times reverted to a 'default state', when the combatants temporarily drew apart.

In the 3rd century BC, towards the start of what we call the Hellenistic period in Greece and the Middle Republic in Rome, for reasons that would repay further study, a change took place in the theory and practice of generalship. Generals were no longer expected in the ordinary run of things to take their place in the front ranks, and few did so. Instead, they began to act as what are often described as 'battle managers'. They moved around, usually on horseback, behind the front line, observing developments, encouraging their men, and issuing tactical orders. Only as a last resort would they now actually fight, and then in such circumstances they often turned to suicide. The changed thinking emerges clearly in the advice given by Philo of Byzantium (c. 200 BC) to a general besieging a city:

> keeping yourself out of range of missiles, or moving along the lines without exposing yourself, exhort the soldiers, distribute praise and honours to those who prove their courage and berate and punish the cowards: in this way all your soldiers will confront danger as well as possible.
>
> (5.4.68–9)

This style of generalship continued through the late Roman Republic and into the empire. Its underlying rationale was well expressed in the 1st century AD by Onasander: 'he can aid his army far less by fighting than he can harm it if he should be killed, since the knowledge of a general is far more important than his physical strength' (33.1). Modern scholarship has hailed Julius Caesar as the epitome of the general as 'battle manager'.

The modern emphasis on 'battle management' might be considered to give a slightly anachronistic slant to our appreciation of generalship in this period. The role of the classical general on the battlefield can be analysed via three categories: the 'physical', actually fighting; the 'practical', issuing tactical orders; and the 'symbolic', actions aimed at altering morale, such as the general riding calmly in the no man's land between the armies, sending away his horse, taking off his helmet, picking up a standard, calling for weapons, and pushing men back into line, or even cutting down a man trying to flee, as well as communicating with the gods, and making formal or off-the-cuff speeches.

We have already seen that the 'physical' was rare, being usually an option of last resort, and then sometimes suicide was preferred. The 'practical', of course, was of undeniable importance, especially in the build-up to fighting. Generals were expected to make great efforts to give battle at the time and place of their choosing. The nature of the terrain was of serious import. Finding a Gallic army drawn up on a hill which was almost completely surrounded by a wide marsh, Caesar overruled the impatience of his troops and refused to give battle (*Gallic War* 7.18–9). The key aspect of the practical side of generalship was drawing up the battle line and issuing orders for pre-planned moves to be made when battle was joined. Seeing the enemy's dispositions on the morning of Pharsalus, Caesar altered his own line of battle and issued instructions on which elements were to charge on what signal (*Civil War* 3.89). Successful impromptu tactical manoeuvres could be ordered during the fighting. At the siege of Alesia, Caesar found a good vantage point from which he sent out a body of reinforcements under Labienus to one point in the fighting, before moving to another spot from which he ordered out two successive bodies to another place in the combat, before leading a third group there in person. That crisis passed, he then ordered some troops to accompany him and others to take a different route to where he had sent Labienus (*Gallic War* 7.85–8). We should not automatically assume that spur of the moment tactical moves were always initiated by the general. His knowledge of the battle was limited to what he could see and hear, and what he was told. At times, others took charge. When outflanked fighting the Helvetii, the third line of the Roman army wheeled to face the new threat. It is notable that Caesar, who is not noted for playing down his own involvement, does not say that he gave the order (*Gallic War* 1.25). We should not take it for granted that all battles contained spontaneous tactical orders. Caesar sometimes 'vanishes' for large portions of his narratives of his own battles (e.g. *Civil War* 3.67–71). It was recognized that a plethora of orders could merely serve to confuse the army, as did Caesar's at the battle of Zela (*Alexandrian War* 75). In some battles, the general's role of 'battle manager' escaped him altogether when the troops ignored them and took matters into their own hands, as Caesar found at Thapsus in Africa (*African War* 80–6).

The 'symbolic' aspect of the general's role was always appropriate, whether in theory or practice, and if things were going well or badly.

If we look again at the passage of Philo of Byzantium quoted above, we see that he highlights the need for the general to raise morale by moving about and speaking to his men. In his presentation of his activities in the latter stages of his victory at Pharsalus, Caesar gives one set of tactical orders but twice makes speeches to encourage the men in what they are already doing (*Civil War* 3.95–7). When things were going very badly indeed at the battle of the Sambre:

> Caesar grabbed a shield from a soldier in the rear ranks (he had come without his own), moved into the front line, spoke to the centurions by name and cheered on the soldiers, ordering the standards to advance and the units to spread out so that they could use their swords more easily. His arrival brought hope to the soldiers and lifted their spirits, each man wanting to do his best under the eyes of his general even in such a desperate situation. So the enemies advance was checked for a while.
>
> (Gallic War 2.25)

Future research may show that a concentration on the 'practical' in the role of the ancient general should not lead us to marginalize the 'symbolic'; that the 'battle management' of the classical commander was as much, if not more, about motivating his men as about tactical finesse.

Chapter 7

'People should know when they are conquered': the reinventions of the Western Way of War

Towards the beginning of the film *Gladiator*, as the Romans wait for the start of the battle, an officer surveys the enemy and says 'People should know when they are conquered'. Maximus the general replies 'Would you, Quintus? Would I?'. As well as calling into question the otherwise rigid distinction between the civilized Romans and the barbaric Germans, this exchange points to the importance of psychological factors in victory and defeat.

In AD 86, after the crushing of a tribal revolt in North Africa, the emperor Domitian is reported to have told the Senate 'I have forbidden the Nasamones to exist'. Cassius Dio, the historian who tells us this, seems to have recorded it as an example of the arrogance of Domitian (67.4.6). The Nasamones continued to exist until the late 3rd century AD, when they were absorbed into the Laguatan confederation of tribes. Although sometimes alleged, genocide was not a practical possibility in the classical world. Most wars, like the one against the Nasamones, were won not by destroying the enemies' practical ability to fight, but by breaking their will to resist.

In 215 BC, during the Second Punic War, Hannibal made an alliance with Philip V, the Antigonid king of Macedon. The terms of the treaty assumed that Rome would continue to exist after the war. Clearly Hannibal thought that his string of victories would bring the Romans to sue for peace on his terms. The Romans, however, in part buoyed up by the fact that the majority of their Italian allies remained loyal, and thus they had a very large reserve of manpower, fought on until it was the Carthaginians who sought peace on Roman terms.

Things were very different between AD 633 and 640, when the Byzantine empire, as the eastern Roman empire after the fall of the west is referred to by modern historians, was stripped of its territories in Syria, and then subsequently, by AD 642, of Egypt, by Arabs under the banner of Islam. It is not easy to account for the Arab conquests. The search for explanations usually proceeds under two headings: Byzantine weaknesses and Arab strengths.

Although they are impossible to quantify, massive economic strain and large-scale loss of manpower had been suffered by the Byzantine empire in a series of wars with Sassanid Persia, which had lasted from AD 604 to 629. The Persians had occupied Syria from AD 614 to 627, and Egypt for ten years from AD 617. Financial stringencies meant that there was a shortage of regular troops for the defence of Syria. There was little tradition of local self-defence in Byzantine Syria. The Byzantines were trying to offset these deficiencies by rebuilding their network of alliances with local non-Muslim Arab allies, which had been wrecked by the Persian occupation, when the Arabs invaded and also began to try to win over the same tribes. It is uncertain to what degree religious divisions in the Byzantine empire undermined its defence. The Monophysite Christians of Syria and Egypt were estranged from, and had been persecuted by, the 'Orthodox' Christians of the Byzantine government. The inhabitants of Syria must at first have seen the Arabs as a barbarous threat. But for those lucky enough

'People should know when they are conquered'

113

not to be killed in one of the towns sacked by the invaders, they would find that their new rulers largely granted freedom of worship on payment of a poll tax. While there is no evidence for local Monophysites aiding the Arabs in Syria, there is some for their involvement in Egypt. Years of Persian rule had shown that Byzantine authority was not an inevitability, and deals done by the locals with the Persians set a precedent for dealing with the Arabs.

Islam had put in place a new ideology and political structure, including the emergence of an elite of settled Arabs from the Quraish clan, which turned Arab martial prowess from traditional inter-tribal wars to the outside world. Islam forbade fighting other Muslims. External aggression may have been particularly apposite after the civil wars known as the *Ridda*, or Apostasy, wars (AD 632–3) which followed the death of the prophet Muhammad. These seem to have left the Arabian peninsular full of armed bands, and to have caused economic dislocation, which could be remedied by booty. Arab successes cannot be put down to superior numbers, since at some battles they seem to have been outnumbered, or to superior weaponry, in which they appear to have been less well supplied than their opponents. Arab success in battle seems to stem from high morale instilled by religious fervour. Every man who fell in battle was to go straight to paradise.

The Byzantine defeat at the battle of Yarmuk in AD 636 was recognized as a turning point. After that, the Byzantines evacuated Syria, began to reorganize their military forces, and tried to create a wasteland on the borders between their neighbouring territory of Cilicia and Syria. There were no sustained attempts to recapture Syria. The defeat of Yarmuk was recognized as irrevocable.

The high costs of recruiting, equipping, and training regular troops had led the Byzantines by the start of the 7th century AD to begin to avoid open battle, in favour of strategic manoeuvre and ambush.

The defeat at Yarmuk strongly reinforced this trend. Yet while the 'Western Way of War' might no longer be much of a reality for the Byzantines, it remained a potent ideology. Later Byzantine historians tended to ascribe the Arab victory at Yarmuk to guile and trickery.

Finally, let us return to where we began, to the battle between the Romans and the Germans at the start of the film *Gladiator*. We can compare and contrast this with another series of visual representations of the same events. One hundred (Roman) feet tall, the Column of Marcus Aurelius in Rome now stands in isolation in the Piazza Colonna, but once was part of an architectural complex, which included a temple of the deified emperor and, probably, a series of colonnades. Commissioned by Commodus, and constructed between AD 180 and 192, the relief sculptures that spiral around the column depict the wars of the emperor's late father, Marcus Aurelius, against the Germans and Sarmatians between AD 172 and 175.

Our purpose here is not to try to see how far the two representations reflect the 'reality' of the wars. Such a project could be considered ultimately fruitless for at least two reasons. Whose 'reality' would we be looking for: that of Marcus, one of his generals or soldiers, that of a Germanic chief or warrior? Also, on the Roman side, at least, it could be thought that all the participants in the wars would have interpreted the reality that confronted them through a filter of their expectations, which, in large part, would have been created by viewing 'war art' similar to the column itself. Instead, here we will think about what the similarities and differences in the depictions tell us about the ways in which a 'Western Way of War' is endlessly reconstructed.

Much remains the same (Figures 11 and 12). The Romans advance to battle in ordered ranks (note how the spears of those in the lower register all slope forward, while those in the higher all slope

11. Column of Marcus Aurelius LXXVIIIa–b

backward), with officers and standards to the front. Their technology is emphasized with their well-detailed equipment, and the pontoon bridge they cross. This is very similar to the disciplined way in which the Romans await the onset of combat in *Gladiator*.

12. Column of Marcus Aurelius XLIII

In battle, the Romans fight hand to hand with calm courage (note their seemingly 'emotionless' faces), and in a communal way (note the close similarity of the poses of the infantrymen). The barbarians, by contrast, either fight with a doomed ferocity (the thrown-back head of the warrior in the centre of the lower register), or flee with panic (the 'despairing' open-handed gesture of the figure in the centre of the upper register). Whatever they do, they do it as individuals (all their poses are different). Again, *Gladiator* echoes these ideas.

Yet much differs in the two depictions. The modern version increases the technological gap between the sides, adding exploding 'Greek fire'-style missiles to the Romans' armoury. The ancient version contains much that is 'suppressed' in the film.

A huge, winged figure of a god comes to the aid of the Romans (Figure 13). From his outstretched arms, torrential rain sweeps the barbarians and their horses into a pile of contorted bodies, while the Romans either are unaffected or shelter under their shields. Gods do not intervene in a 'realistic' modern version of ancient battle.

The Romans sack a village (Figure 14). The barbarian at the top pleads for help from the gods. It will do him no good. We have already seen whose side the gods are on in this contest. At the bottom right, a barbarian who has been knocked to his hands and knees is about to be butchered by a Roman soldier (compare with Chapter 6, the legionary). To the left, a woman and child seek to flee, past the body of a barbarian man (her husband, brother, or father?), but a soldier catches her by the hair. Her clothes have come off her shoulder, revealing her right breast. This points to the rape she has or will suffer. This scene is far from being a regrettable case of the troops getting out of control. The sack is watched over by Marcus himself, backed by his officers and the standards of Rome. 'Ethnic cleansing' such as this finds no place in the modern recreation of the ancient 'Western Way of War'.

Seven women and three children are taken into captivity, and probably slavery (Figure 15). It is conducted in a disciplined way

13. Column of Marcus Aurelius XVI

14. Column of Marcus Aurelius XX

15. Column of Marcus Aurelius CIV

(see the almost identical poses of the two soldiers at the left), but the lower register points to a messier and more distressing interpretation, as the two women are dragged away by soldiers. The clothes of both women are in disarray, and they make palm-outward gestures of unhappiness. Mass rape and enslavement does not feature in *Gladiator*.

Their hands tied behind their backs, two barbarian prisoners are bent forward for execution (Figure 16). At their feet are two earlier victims, whose heads lie beside their slumped bodies. More of the condemned wait their turn on either side. Although Roman cavalry watch over the scene from the rear, it is interesting that the executioners, like their victims, are barbarians. Are the Romans forcing their prisoners to kill each other, or should this be interpreted as indicating the disunity of barbarians? In *Gladiator* Romans finish off wounded barbarians in the immediate aftermath of battle, but there is no hint of mass killings of prisoners in cold blood.

Marcus Aurelius, known in other contexts, both in antiquity and today, as the 'philosopher emperor', sits as his troops bring captives before him (Figure 17). One soldier, however, presents the emperor with a severed head. *Gladiator* reverses this motif. Head-hunting in the film is confined to the barbarians.

The column is full of fighting, but for the ancient observer, no matter how carefully or briefly they viewed its scenes, or from what angle, or in what order, there was no suspense. They already knew how the story ended. For they had seen, as we cannot, the now destroyed sculptures nearest to eye level on the base (Figure 18). Known to us via a drawing from AD c. 1540, the east side of the base gave away the ending. To the left stood the emperor, while to the right Roman soldiers keep an eye on barbarians, who kneel and make gestures of submission. Unlike the barbarians in *Gladiator*, these barbarians know when they are conquered.

16. Column of Marcus Aurelius LXI

17. Column of Marcus Aurelius LXVI

The similarities and the differences between the visualizations of the same battles on the ancient column of Marcus and in the modern film *Gladiator* illustrate how the 'Western Way of War' is constantly reinvented.

Out of the reality of the Persian Wars, the Greeks constructed the nexus of ideas that we label the 'Western Way of War'. In this concept the Westerners' ultimate goal in war is a pitched battle which aspires to annihilate the enemy. Preferably it is fought hand to hand by heavy infantry. Victory comes from courage, and this stems partly from training and discipline, and partly from 'civic

COL. ANTONINI

18. Column of Marcus Aurelius, east face of base

militarism', the combatants being landowners who have political freedom. This was always more of an ideology than an objective reality.

In no period were all the elements of the 'Western Way of War' in place. Paradoxically, the time that might be thought to most closely approach the ideal was the Greek world between the introduction of the hoplite phalanx and the Persian Wars. Yet, as we have seen, we know little about war in this period, and there is a temptation to simplify and project back into this era what we know of later practices. The stress in the ideology on free men fighting the non-free appears to have come about as a result of Greek perceptions of the Persian Wars, and it should be remembered that many hoplites in Greek *polis* armies in the years between c. 725 and 490 BC probably had little or no political freedom in the classical senses of equality before the law and a right to participate in political decision-making. For long periods of time, very few of the ideas that make up the concept of the 'Western Way of War' have been present in the reality of Western European war-making. For example, the historian John Lynn has demonstrated that 'civic militarism', with some partial exceptions, disappeared with the fall of the Roman Republic at the end of the 1st century BC and did not reappear until the French Revolution at the end of the 18th century AD. A gap of some 1,800 years in a supposed continuity of 2,500 years does not make for much of a proposition.

While there was little continuity of practice, the ideology of a 'Western Way of War' proved both tenacious and extremely flexible. Various Western societies looked back to the Greeks and Romans and thought either that they should fight in the style classical authors admired, or, with remarkable intellectual slight of hand, that they actually did. An important text in the transmission of classical ideas about war was Vegetius' *Epitoma rei militaris*. Writing some time between AD 383 and 450, Vegetius mixed past and present practices with wishful thinking to build a prescriptive programme for late Roman warfare. Vegetius moves in the realm of theory rather than reflecting contemporary reality. Much of Vegetius fits squarely in the 'Western Way of War', both his emphasis on training and discipline leading to courage (e.g. 1.1; 28) and his ethnographic view of the world – Germans are big, Africans treacherous, people from the cold north stupid, those from the hot south cowardly, and so on (1.1–2). Yet the ideology has been adapted from that of the past. Writing in the aftermath of the crushing defeat of the Roman army by the Goths at Adrianople in AD 378, Vegetius advises generals to be wary of open battle, instead they should aim to ambush the enemy (3.9). If the 'Western Way of War' could be remodelled by Vegetius in late antiquity, this was nothing compared to the changes that would be made to it later. Vegetius was admired in the Middle Ages in Western Europe. But he was not read as a blueprint for change, but as a reaffirmation of contemporary practices. Centralizing Vegetius' words on courage, the medieval European nobility interpreted Vegetius' work as a handbook on chivalry. In one edition, it even acquired the title *'Livre de chevalerie'*.

The 'Western Way of War', however, has not always served just to put a gloss on contemporary reality; at times it has been used to alter it. Starting in the late 16th century, the Dutch general Maurice of Nassau drew on classical models to drill and form up armies, and the citizen soldier of Republican Rome was an inspiration throughout the 18th century, which culminated in the armies of the French Revolution.

An uncritical acceptance of the ever-changing ideology of the 'Western Way of War' as an objective reality, the belief that there is a genuine continuity of practices between the ancient Greeks and the modern West, could have two dangerous results. First, it might lead to complacency in the West. The thinking could run on the lines, 'ever since the Greeks inspired by "civic militarism" sought decisive combat the West has been ultimately successful in war; providing the West's approach to war-making remains essentially the same, it will always win.' As such, this could serve much the same function of an 'ideological comfort blanket' as did the classical cultures' beliefs that barbarians did not change, and newly encountered ones were just the same old ones with a new name; beaten before, they would be again. The second dangerous result might be an abandoning, or weakening, of restraints on war-making by the West. This thinking could run, 'it is the nature of the "Western Way of War" to seek to annihilate the enemy, so a Western state that takes any action to lead to this result is just being true to its nature.' This could operate in a similarly pernicious way to the Greeks' ideas that wars against barbarians do not need restraint because it is the nature of barbarians to be slaves.

It is much better, and safer, to see the 'Western Way of War' for what it is: a long-lived, highly adaptable, and powerful ideology. The 'Western Way of War' is constantly reinvented, as, of course, it has been in this book.

Further reading

Popular, illustrated introductions are P. Connolly, *Greece and Rome at War* (London, 1981); A. K. Goldsworthy, *Roman Warfare* (London, 2000); J. Hackett (ed.), *Warfare in the Ancient World* (London, 1989); V. D. Hanson, *The Wars of the Ancient Greeks* (London, 1999); and J. Warry, *Warfare in the Classical World* (London, 1980). Osprey Publishing produce short books on specific aspects of ancient war that are aimed at a popular readership, these are always well illustrated and the best have an informed text, for example B. Rankov, *The Praetorian Guard* (Oxford, 1994); and M. Whitby, *Rome at War* AD 293–696 (Oxford, 2002).

The Cambridge History of Greek and Roman Warfare, edited by P. Sabin, H. van Wees, and M. Whitby, forthcoming in two volumes, will provide the standard textbook. The five volumes of W. K. Pritchett, *The Greek State at War* (Berkeley and Los Angeles, 1971–91) give an exhaustive survey of the Greek evidence.

Almost all the relevant ancient texts are available in the Loeb series (original on left-hand page with English translation on right) published by Harvard University Press, and most are translated into English in Penguin Classics or Oxford World's Classics.

The Oxford Classical Dictionary (3rd edn, Oxford, 1996), edited by S. Hornblower, and A. Spawforth, is essential for all research into the ancient world. It is the source of the standard abbreviations used to refer to classical texts.

Preface

The concept of the 'Western Way of War' was first sketched in V. D. Hanson, *The Western Way of War: Infantry Battle in Ancient Greece* (Oxford, 1989). It is carried further in V. D. Hanson, *Why the West has Won: Carnage and Culture from Salamis to Vietnam* (London, 2001). It is accepted by J. Keegan, *A History of Warfare* (London, 1993); but rejected by J. A. Lynn, *Battle: A History of Combat and Culture from Ancient Greece to Modern America* (Boulder, Colorado, and Oxford, 2003).

A splendid introduction to the Neo-Assyrian empire is A. Kuhrt, *The Ancient Near East c.3000–330 BC* (2 vols, London and New York, 1995), pp. 473–546. A brief introduction to Assyrian war is given by A. K. Grayson, in J. Boardman, I. E. S. Edwards, N. G. L. Hammond, E. Sollberger, and C. B. F. Walker (eds), *The Cambridge Ancient History, Volume III* (2nd edn, Cambridge, 1991), pp. 217–21. A longer study is F. Malbran-Labat, *L'Armée et L'Orginisation Militaire de L'Assyrie d'après les lettres des Sargonides trouvées à Ninive* (Paris, 1982). Also to be consulted is Y. Yadin, *The Art of Warfare in Biblical Lands in the Light of Archaeological Discovery* (London, 1963), pp. 291–328, with plates at pp. 380–463. A popular, unannotated but well-illustrated, overview of the Assyrian army can be found in N. Stillman and N. Tallis, *Armies of the Ancient Near East 3000 BC to 539 BC* (Worthing, 1984).

A classic study of changes in the concept of freedom within one culture is C. Wirszubski, *Libertas as a Political Idea at Rome during the Late Republic and Early Empire* (Cambridge, 1950).

The Hjortspring find is discussed by K. Randsborg, 'Into the Iron Age: a discourse on war and society', in *Ancient Warfare: Archaeological Perspectives*, edited by J. Carman and A. Harding (Stroud, 1999), pp. 191–202.

On the Zulus, see below, under Chapter 3.

For the Peloponnesian War, Thucydides is our main source. S. Hornblower, *The Greek World 479–323 BC* (revised edn, London and New York, 1991) gives a succinct account. The battles referred to in the text are Delion (424 BC), Mantinea (418 BC), and (the uncertain example) Amphipolis (422 BC). See Tacitus, *Annals* 1.49–2.26 on Germanicus' campaigns; Caesar, *Civil War* 3.39–73 on Dyrrachium; and Tacitus, *Agricola* 29–38 on Mons Graupius.

For concise overviews of the age of Justinian and the eastern Roman army, see respectively the contributions by A. Cameron, pp. 63–85; and M. Whitby, pp. 300–14, in A. Cameron, B. Ward-Perkins, and M. Whitby (eds), *The Cambridge Ancient History, Volume XIV* (2nd edn, Cambidge, 2000). Also accessible are A. Cameron, *Procopius and the Sixth Century* (London, 1985); and J. Moorhead, *Justinian* (London and New York, 1994). A popular, well-illustrated work is R. Boss, *Justinian's Wars: Belisarius, Narses and the Reconquest of the West* (Stockport, 1993).

Chapter 1
Greeks and Trojans
On the absence of a judgemental Greek/barbarian divide in Homer, and its creation with the Persian Wars, see E. Hall, *Inventing the Barbarian. Greek Self-Definition through Tragedy* (Oxford, 1989). More on Homer: H. S. Mackie, *Talking Trojan: Speech and Community in the Iliad* (Lanham, Md., 1996); and C. F. Salazar, *The Treatment of Wounds in Graeco-Roman Antiquity* (Leiden, Boston, and Köln, 2000), pp. 126–58. For a reconstruction, see H. van Wees, 'Homeric Warfare', in *A New Companion to Homer*, edited by I. Morris and B. Powell (Leiden, New York, and Köln, 1997), pp. 668–93; and below, Chapter 3, the 'Hoplite Revolution' in Greece.

Greeks and Persians
On the rise of the *polis*, see R. Osborne, *Greece in the Making 1200–479 BC* (London and New York, 1996). On Persian armies, see P. Briant, 'The

Further reading

131

Achaemenid Empire', in *War and Society in the Ancient and Medieval Worlds*, edited by K. Raaflaub and N. Rosenstein (Cambridge, Mass., and London, 1999), pp. 105–28; and D. Head, *The Achaemenid Persian Army* (Stockport, 1992). On the course of the Persian Wars, see J. F. Lazenby, *The Defence of Greece* (Warminster, 1993); on Herodotus and (Ps.-)Hippocrates, P. Cartledge, *The Greeks: A Portrait of Self and Others* (Oxford, 1993), pp. 36–62; on Aeschylus, E. Hall, 'Asia unmanned: Images of victory in Classical Athens', in *War and Society in the Greek World*, edited by J. Rich and G. Shipley (London and New York, 1993), pp. 108–33; and on positive cultural interactions, M. C. Miller, *Athens and Persia in the Fifth Century BC* (Cambridge, 1997).

Romans and Carthaginians

On early Rome, see T. J. Cornell, *The Beginnings of Rome* (London and New York, 1995); on Punic Wars, B. M. Caven, *The Punic Wars* (London, 1980); on expansionism, H. Sidebottom, 'Roman Imperialism: the changed outward trajectory of the Roman empire', *Historia* (forthcoming); on the Carthaginian army, G. Daly, *Cannae: The Experience of Battle in the Second Punic War* (London and New York, 2002); on the ethnographic stereotype of Carthaginians, J. P. V. D. Balsdon, *Romans and Aliens* (London, 1979) and S. Lancel, *Hannibal* (Oxford, 1999), pp. 216–21; on the Punic world view, R. Batty, 'Mela's Phoenician Geography', *Journal of Roman Studies*, 90 (2000), pp. 70–94; and on Septimius Severus, A. R. Birley, *The African Emperor Septimius Severus* (3rd edn, London, 1988).

Romans and Greeks

On the Roman conquest of the Greek east, see E. S. Gruen, *The Hellenistic World and the Coming of Rome* (Berkeley, Los Angeles, and London, 1984); on Hellenization, M. Beard and M. Crawford, *Rome in the Late Republic* (London, 1985), pp. 12–24; and on Roman views of Greeks, J. P. V. D. Balsdon, *Romans and Aliens* (London, 1979), especially pp. 30–58.

Art and the 'Western Way of War'

The crater is illustrated in J. Hackett (ed.), *Warfare in the Ancient World* (London, 1989), p. 73.

Wonderful introductions to classical art are provided by R. Osborne, *Archaic and Classical Greek Art* (Oxford, 1998); N. Spivey, *Greek Art* (London, 1997); M. Beard and J. Henderson, *Classical Art: From Greece to Rome* (Oxford, 2001); and J. Elsner, *Imperial Rome and Christian Triumph* (Oxford, 1998).

Oddly, there are no modern book-length and systematic studies of Greek and Roman 'war art'. For shorter studies, see the contributions by L. Hannestad, pp. 110–119, and N. Hannestad, pp. 146–54, in T. Bekker-Nielsen and L. Hannestad (eds), *War as a Cultural and Social Force: Essays on Warfare in Antiquity* (Copenhagen, 2001); and T. Hölscher, 'Images of war in Greece and Rome: between military practice, public memory, and cultural symbolism', *Journal of Roman Studies*, 93 (2003), pp. 1–17. See also H. Sidebottom, *Fields of Mars: A Cultural History of Greek and Roman Battle* (London, forthcoming.)

Chapter 2
Culture

On the Bridgeness Slab, see L. J. F. Keppie and B. J. Arnold, *Corpus Signorum Imperii Romani. Great Britain. Volume 1.4. Scotland* (Oxford, 1984), pp. 27–8 (no. 68), plate 21; and I. M. Ferris, *Enemies of Rome: Barbarians through Roman Eyes* (Stroud, 2000), pp. 113–18.

For the *Brittunculi* tablet, see A. K. Bowman and J. D. Thomas, *The Vindolanda Writing-Tablets* (London, 1994), pp. 106–108 (no. 164). The world of the tablets is reconstructed by A. R. Birley, *Garrison Life at Vindolanda* (Stroud, 2002).

The standard edition of the *Agricola* is by R. M. Ogilvie and I. A. Richmond (Oxford, 1967). A stimulating recent interpretation is K. Clarke, 'An island nation: re-reading Tacitus' Agricola', *Journal of Roman Studies*, 91 (2001), pp. 94–112.

On classical images of 'northerners', see A. N. Sherwin-White, *Racial Prejudice in Imperial Rome* (Cambridge, 1967), pp. 1–61; and for 'nomads', B. D. Shaw, '"Eaters of Flesh, Drinkers of Milk": The ancient Mediterranean ideology of the pastoral nomad', *Ancient society*, 13/14 (1982/83), pp. 5–31.

P. Heather, *The Goths* (Oxford and Cambridge, Mass., 1996), pp. 51–93, discusses changes in German tribes.

On identifying Huns with earlier barbarians, see J. O. Maenchen-Helfen, *The World of the Huns* (Berkeley, Los Angeles, and London, 1973), pp. 1–17; and J. Matthews, *The Roman Empire of Ammianus* (London, 1989), pp. 332–42; 353–5.

The 5th century AD survival of ethnographic thinking in the West is examined by P. Heather, 'The barbarian in late antiquity: image, reality, and transformation', in R. Miles (ed.), *Constructing Identities in Late Antiquity* (London and New York, 1999), pp. 234–58.

On ideology on the eastern front, see O. Bartov, *Hitler's Army: Soldiers, Nazis, and War in the Third Reich* (Oxford, 1992).

Gender

Introductions to modern scholarship are provided by D. Montserrat, 'Reading gender in the Roman world', in J. Huskinson (ed.), *Experiencing Rome* (London and New York, 2000), pp. 153–81; and D. H. J. Larmour, P. A. Miller, and C. Platter (eds), *Rethinking Sexuality: Foucault and Classical Antiquity* (Princeton, 1998), pp. 3–41.

For women and war, see S. Hornblower, 'War and the development of ancient historiography', in P. Sabin, H. van Wees, and M. Whitby (eds), *The Cambridge History of Greek and Roman Warfare* (Cambridge, forthcoming). J. K. Evans, *War, Women and Children in Ancient Rome* (London and New York, 1991) is interested in the indirect social and economic effects of warfare.

Amazons are studied by K. Dowden, 'The Amazons: development and functions', *Rheinisches Museum für Philologie*, 140 (1997), pp. 97–128.

On the Nereid Monument, see W. A. P. Childs and P. Demargue, *Fouilles de Xanthos*, VIII (Paris, 1989).

The references for women and sieges are: Plataea, Thucydides 2.78; Byzantium, Cassius Dio 75.12.4; Chios, Plutarch, *The Bravery of Women* 244E–254C; Argos (physically fighting), Plutarch, *The Bravery of Women* 245C–F; Argos (throwing roof tiles), Plutarch, *Pyrrhus* 34.1–2; Rome, Livy 1.11.

For masculinity and war, see H. van Wees, 'Warfare and society', in P. Sabin, H. van Wees, and M. Whitby (eds), *The Cambridge History of Greek and Roman Warfare* (Cambridge, forthcoming); and D. Ogden, 'Homosexuality and warfare in ancient Greece', in A. B. Lloyd (ed.), *Battle in Antiquity* (London and Swansea, 1996), pp. 107–68.

A recent reinterpretation of the *Kinaidos* by J. Davidson, *Courtesans and Fishcakes* (London, 1998), pp. 167–82, plays up the insatiability and marginalizes the passivity.

The individual
J. Griffin, *Latin Poets and Roman Life* (London, 1985) is a modern classic. Specifically on lovers as soldiers, see M. R. Gale, 'Propertius 2.7: *Militia Amoris* and the ironics of Elegy', *Journal of Roman Studies*, 87 (1997), pp. 77–91.

On philosophers as soldiers, see H. Sidebottom, 'Philosophers' attitudes to warfare under the principate', in J. Rich and G. Shipley (eds), *War and Society in the Roman World* (London and New York, 1993), pp. 241–64.

On early Christianity, R. Lane Fox, *Pagans and Christians* (Harmonsworth, 1986) is a splendid guide. On soldiers of Christ, see A. Harnack, *Militia Christi: The Christian Religion and the*

Military in the First Three Centuries (English tr., Philadelphia, 1981), pp. 27–64.

D. E. E. Kleiner, *Roman Sculpture* (New Haven and London, 1992), pp. 256–9; 301–8; 350–1; 384–92; 455–9, provides a wonderful introduction to sarcophagi, with discussion of the Portonaccio Sarcophagus at pp. 301–3; see also J. Elsner, *Imperial Rome and Christian Triumph* (Oxford and New York, 1998), pp. 145–58, for an interpretation closer to that offered in this book.

On the militarization of the Roman civil service, see R. MacMullen, *Soldier and Civilian in the Later Roman Empire* (Cambridge, Mass., 1963), pp. 163–5; 171–2.

Chapter 3

On Zulus, D. R. Morris, *The Washing of the Spears: The Rise and Fall of the Zulu Nation* (revised edn, London, 1989) is a classic narrative. R. Edgerton, *Like Lions They Fought: The Zulu War and the Last Black Empire in South Africa* (New York, 1988) is particularly good on the actualities of combat. See also J. Keegan, *A History of Warfare* (London, 1993), pp. 28–32; and W. S. Ferguson, 'The Zulus and the Spartans: a comparison of their military systems', *Harvard African Studies*, 2 (1918), pp. 197–234.

The 'hoplite revolution' in Greece

For the Athenian oinochoe, see G. Ahlberg, *Fighting on Land and Sea in Geometric Art* (Stockholm, 1971), pp. 12–13; and for the 'Chigi vase', P. Arias, B. Shefton, and M. Hirmer, *A History of Vase Painting* (London, 1962), pp. 275–6.

On New Guinea, see R. Gardner and K. G. Heider, *Gardens of War: Life and Death in the New Guinea Stone Age* (Harmondsworth, 1974).

Antony Andrewes' views are set out in his *The Greek Tyrants* (London, 1956), especially pp. 31–8. Among others who see a revolution/ significant reform are A. M. Snodgrass, 'The Hoplite Reform and history', *Journal of Hellenic Studies*, 86 (1965), pp. 110–22; P. Cartledge, 'Hoplites and heroes: Sparta's contribution to the technique of ancient warfare', *Journal of Hellenic Studies*, 97 (1977), pp. 11–27; and J. Salmon, 'Political Hoplites?', *Journal of Hellenic Studies*, 97 (1977), pp. 84–101.

The arguments of Joachim Latacz are found in *Kampfparänese, Kampfdarstellung und Kampfwirklichkeit in der Ilias, bei Kallinos und Tyrtaios* (Munich, 1977). Among other 'revisionist' views are K. A. Raaflaub, 'Soldiers, citizens, and the evolution of the early Greek *Polis*', in L. G. Mitchell and P. J. Rhodes (eds), *The Development of the Polis in Archaic Greece* (London and New York, 1997), pp. 49–59; and H. van Wees, 'The development of the Hoplite phalanx: iconography and reality in the seventh century', in H. van Wees (ed.), *War and Violence in Archaic Greece* (London and Swansea, 2000), pp. 125–66.

Re-argued 'orthodoxy' is found in A. M. Snodgrass, 'The "Hoplite reform" revisited', *Dialogues d'histoire ancienne*, 19.1 (1993), pp. 47–61; and P. A. Cartledge, 'The birth of the Hoplite: Sparta's contribution to early Greek military organization', in P. A. Cartledge (ed.), *Spartan Reflections* (London, 2001), pp. 153–66.

Callinus and Tyrtaeus can be found in M. L. West, *Greek Lyric Poetry* (Oxford, 1993).

Change of thinking: burials, D. C. Kurtz and J. Boardman, *Greek Burial Customs* (London, 1971), pp. 207–8; dedications, A. M. Snodgrass, *Archaic Greece: The Age of Experiment* (Berkely and Los Angeles, 1980), pp. 105–7; and A. J. B. Wace, 'Lead figurines', in R. M. Dawkins (ed.), *The Sanctuary of Artemis Orthia at Sparta* (London, 1929), pp. 249–84.

The 'agrarian crisis' in Italy

The 'traditional view' is well set out in K. Hopkins, *Conquerors and Slaves: Sociological Studies in Roman History* (Cambridge, 1978), pp. 1–75; 102–6; also, briefly, in B. Cunliffe, *Greeks, Romans and Barbarians: Spheres of Interaction* (London, 1988), pp. 59–79.

Attacks on the above: J. K. Evans, '*Plebs Rustica*: the peasantry of classical Italy', *American Journal of Ancient History*, 5 (1980), pp. 19–47; J. W. Rich, 'The supposed manpower shortage of the later second century BC', *Historia*, 32 (1983), pp. 287–331; and S. L. Dyson, *Community and Society in Roman Italy* (Baltimore and London, 1992), pp. 23–55.

On demography, see N. Morley, 'The transformation of Italy, 225–28 BC', *Journal of Roman Studies*, 91 (2001), pp. 50–62.

On Tiberius Graccus and archaeology in Etruria, see respectively D. Stockton, *The Gracchi* (Oxford, 1979), pp. 6–22; and T. W. Potter, *The Changing Landscape of South Etruria* (London, 1979), pp. 120–37.

An overview of the debate is given by N. Rosenstein, 'Republican Rome', in K. Raaflaub and N. Rosenstein (eds), *War and Society in the Ancient and Medieval Worlds* (Cambridge, Mass., and London, 1999), pp. 205–10.

The 'barbarization' of the Roman army

All modern work on the late Roman army is indebted to A. H. M. Jones, *The Later Roman Empire 284–602* (Oxford, 1964), pp. 607–86.

Two important revisionist works are H. Elton, *Warfare in Roman Europe AD 350–425* (Oxford, 1996); and M. J. Nicasie, *Twilight of Empire: The Roman Army from the Reign of Diocletian until the Battle of Adrianople* (Amsterdam, 1998).

More traditional interpretations, although none of them hold the simplified popular view outlined at the start of this section, include A. Ferrill, *The Fall of the Roman Empire: The Military Explanation* (London, 1986); W. Liebeschuetz, 'The end of the Roman army in the western empire', in J. Rich and G. Shipley (eds), *War and Society in the Roman World* (London and New York, 1993), pp. 265–76; and R. MacMullen, *Corruption and the Decline of Rome* (New Haven and London, 1988).

An exploration of why the east survived while the west fell is provided by S. Williams and G. Friell, *The Rome That Did Not Fall: The Survival of the East in the Fifth Century* (London, 1999).

Why do historical interpretations change?

For some speculations on this area, see M. J. Nicasie, *Twilight of Empire: The Roman Army from the Reign of Diocletian until the Battle of Adrianople* (Amsterdam, 1998), p. 97, n.1; and P. A. Cartledge, 'The birth of the Hoplite: Sparta's contribution to early Greek military organization', in P. A. Cartledge (ed.), *Spartan Reflections* (London, 2001), p. 156.

Chapter 4

See R. Sorabji, 'Take time to win the philosophical battle', *The Times Higher Education Supplement*, 9 May 2003, p. 16.

Classical Greeks

D. Dawson, *The Origins of Western Warfare* (Boulder, Colorado, and Oxford, 1996), provides an accessible synopsis of Greek (as well as Roman) ideologies of war, although with more stress on the systematic (for the Greeks) than is given in the text here.

Also useful are A. Momigliano, 'Some observations on causes of war in ancient historiography', in A. Momigliano (ed.), *Studies in Historiography* (London, 1966), pp. 112–26; J. Cobet, 'Herodotus and Thucydides on war', in I. S. Moxon, J. D. Smart, and A. J. Woodman (eds), *Past Perspectives: Studies in Greek and Roman Historical Writing* (Cambridge, 1986), pp. 1–18; M. Defourny, 'The aim of the state: peace', in J. Barnes, M. Schofield, and R. Sorabji (eds), *Articles on Aristotle 2: Ethics and Politics* (London, 1977), pp. 195–201; and H. van Wees, 'Warfare and society', in P. Sabin, H. van Wees, and M. Whitby (eds), *The Cambridge History of Greek and Roman Warfare* (Cambridge, forthcoming).

Republican Romans

The two standard works, both in German, on the Roman 'just war' are

S. Albert, *Bellum iustum: Die Theorie des 'gerechten Krieges' und ihre praktische Bedeutung für die auswärtigen Auseinandersetzungen Roms in republikanischer Zeit* (Kallmunz, 1980); and M. Mantovani, *Bellum iustum: Die Idee des gerechten Krieges in der römischen Kaiserzeit* (Bern, 1990). See also P. A. Brunt, 'Laus Imperii', in P. A. Brunt (ed.), *Roman Imperial Themes* (Oxford, 1990), pp. 288–323; and H. Sidebottom, 'War, peace, and international relations', in P. Sabin, H. van Wees, and M. Whitby (eds), *The Cambridge History of Greek and Roman Warfare* (Cambridge, forthcoming).

On the *Fetiales*, see M. Beard, J. North, and S. Price, *Religions of Rome* (Cambridge, 1998).

Civil war

On stasis in the Greek world, see A. Lintott, *Violence, Civil Strife and Revolution in the Classical City* (London and Canberra, 1982); and H.-J. Gehrke, *Stasis: Untersuchungen zu den inneren Kriegen in den griechischen Staaten des 5. und 4. Jahrhunderts v. Chr.* (Munich, 1985).

An informative discussion of Thucydides on Corcyra is W. R. Connor, *Thucydides* (Princeton, 1984), pp. 95–105.

A good introduction to the conspiracy of Catiline is E. Rawson, *Cicero: A Portrait* (London, 1983), pp. 60–88.

J. Henderson, *Fighting For Rome: Poets and Caesars, History and Civil War* (Cambridge, 1998) is a fascinating, if challenging, read on Roman thinking about civil wars in general.

Greeks under Rome

Greek theories are studied by H. Sidebottom, 'Philosophers' attitudes to warfare under the principate', in J. Rich and G. Shipley (eds), *War and Society in the Roman World* (London and New York, 1993), pp. 241–64. For a somewhat different interpretation, see D. Dawson, *The Origins of Western Warfare* (Boulder, Colorado, and Oxford, 1996), pp. 132–8.

Christians under Rome

In general, see R. H. Bainton, *Christian Attitudes Towards War and Peace: A Historical Survey and Critical Re-evaluation* (London, 1961).

H. Chadwick, *Augustine* (Oxford, 1986) provides an introduction; for specifics, see L. J. Swift, 'Augustine on war and killing: another view', *Harvard Theological Review*, 66 (1973), pp. 369–83; and for later influence, J. Barnes, 'The Just War', in N. Kretzmann, A. Kenny, and J. Pinborg (eds), *The Cambridge History of Later Medieval Philosophy* (Cambridge, 1982), pp. 771–84.

Chapter 5
Strategies or fantasies?

As far as I know there is no modern discussion of classical ideas of unfulfilled schemes of huge conquests as a phenomenon. For views on the individual examples cited in the text, see D. Kagan, *The Peace of Nicias and the Sicilian Expedition* (Ithaca and London, 1981), pp. 170–3; 248–50; R. Lane Fox, *Alexander the Great* (London, 1973), pp. 475–80; M. Gelzer, *Caesar: Politician and Statesman* (English tr., Oxford, 1968), p. 322; B. C. McGing, *The Foreign Policy of Mithridates VI Eupator King of Pontus* (Leiden, 1986), pp. 164–5; and (on Sassanid kings) D. S. Potter, *Prophecy and History in the Crisis of the Roman Empire* (Oxford, 1990), pp. 370–80.

Further reading

S. P. Mattern, *Rome and the Enemy* (Berkeley and Los Angeles, 1999), pp. 41–66, provides a good introduction to classical geography and strategy. The concept of 'odological thinking' was pioneered by P. Janni, *La Mappa e il Periplo: Cartografia Antica e Spazio Odologico* (Rome, 1984).

A 'grand strategy' for the Roman empire?

E. N. Luttwak, *The Grand Strategy of the Roman Empire* (Baltimore and London, 1976).

Two contributions which, more or less, support Luttwak are A. Ferrill, *Roman Imperial Grand Strategy* (New York, 1991); and E. L. Wheeler,

'Methodological limits and the mirage of Roman strategy', *Journal of Military History*, 57 (1993), pp. 7–41; 215–40, the latter pointing out that Luttwak's arguments, at times, are misrepresented by his critics.

Among the attacks on Luttwak's ideas are J. C. Mann, 'Power, force and the frontiers of the empire', *Journal of Roman Studies*, 69 (1979), pp. 175–83; F. Millar, 'Emperors, frontiers and foreign relations, 31 BC to AD 378', *Britannia*, 13 (1982), pp. 1–23; B. Isaac, *The Limits of Empire: The Roman Army in the East* (Oxford, 1990); and C. R. Whittaker, *Frontiers of the Roman Empire* (Baltimore and London, 1994).

Campaigns and logistics: some general considerations

A stimulating introduction to the topics discussed in this section, and to much else, is Y. Garlan, *War in the Ancient World* (English tr., London, 1975).

On the Colosseum being paid for by booty, see G. Alföldy, 'Eine Bauinschrift aus dem Colosseum', *Zeitschrift für Papyrologie und Epigraphik*, 109 (1995), pp. 195–226.

On the economics of war and military pay, see the contributions of V. Gabrielsen, D. W. Rathbone, and D. Lee to *The Cambidge History of Greek and Roman Warfare*, edited by P. Sabin, H. van Wees, and M. Whitby (Cambridge, forthcoming).

Academic studies of mercenaries include H. W. Parke, *Greek Mercenary Soldiers from the Earliest Times to the Battle of Ipsus* (Oxford, 1933); G. T. Griffith, *Mercenaries of the Hellenistic World* (Cambridge, 1935); and M. Bettalli, *I Mercenari nel mondo Greco. I. Dalle origini alla fine del V sec. A. C.* (Pisa, 1995). A popular overview is S. Yalichev, *Mercenaries of the Ancient World* (London, 1997).

A good introduction to logistics is J. P. Roth, 'War in the Hellenistic World and Roman Republic', in P. Sabin, H. van Wees, and M. Whitby (eds), *The Cambridge History of Greek and Roman Warfare*

(Cambridge, forthcoming). The book-length studies mentioned in the text are D. W. Engels, *Alexander the Great and the Logistics of the Macedonian Army* (Berkeley, Los Angeles, and London, 1978); P. Erdkamp, *Hunger and the Sword: Warfare and Food Supply in Roman Republican Wars* (Amsterdam, 1998); and J. P. Roth, *The Logistics of the Roman Army at War (264 BC–AD 235)* (Leiden, Boston, and Koln, 1999).

On marching camps in Scotland, see C. M. Gilliver, *The Roman Art of War* (Stroud and Charleston, SC, 1999).

Campaigns and logistics: 'unhorsing the Huns'

See R. P. Lindner, 'Nomadism, horses and Huns', *Past and Present*, 92 (1981), pp. 3–19.

A scholar who follows Lindner is C. R. Whittaker, *Frontiers of the Roman Empire* (Baltimore and London, 1994), p. 214. See E. L. Wheeler, 'Methodolical limits and the mirage of Roman strategy', *Journal of Military History*, 57 (1993), pp. 15–16, for a dissenting voice.

On the Huns in general, see E. A. Thompson, *The Huns* (Oxford and Cambridge, Mass., 1996) for history, and I. Bóna, *Das Hunnenreich* (Stuttgart, 1991) for archaeology, as well as the works cited above under Chapter 2, Culture.

Chapter 6

See J. Keegan, *The Face of Battle: A Study of Agincourt, Waterloo and the Somme* (London, 1976).

Far and away the best subsequent study of this field is R. Holmes, *Firing Line* (London, 1985; now republished as *Acts of War*, London, 2003).

An exploration of the experience of classical warriors in combat is a central theme of H. Sidebottom, *Fields of Mars: A Cultural History of Greek and Roman Battle* (London, forthcoming).

The hoplite

On the statuette of the hoplite, see H. van Wees, 'The development of the Hoplite phalanx: iconography and reality in the seventh century', in H. van Wees (ed.), *War and Violence in Ancient Greece* (London and Swansea, 2000), pp. 129–31.

Two books by A. M. Snodgrass are essential for hoplite equipment: *Early Greek Armour and Weapons from the End of the Bronze Age to 600 BC* (Edinburgh, 1964); and *Arms and Armour of the Greeks* (London, 1967).

For the commonly accepted view of hoplite battle: V. D. Hanson, *The Western Way of War: Infantry Battle in Ancient Greece* (Oxford, 1989). Other views: G. L. Cawkwell, *Philip of Macedon* (London, 1978); and A. K. Goldsworthy, 'The Othismos, myths and heresies: the nature of Hoplite battle', *War in History*, 4.1 (1997), pp. 1–26.

The phalangite

Good introductions to Macedonian and Hellenistic war-making, respectively, are A. B. Bosworth, *Conquest and Empire* (Cambridge, 1988), especially pp. 259–77; and Y. Garlan, 'War and siegecraft', in F. W. Walbank and A. E. Astin (eds), *The Cambridge Ancient History*, 7.1 (2nd edn, Cambridge, 1984), pp. 353–62.

N. Sekunda, *The Army of Alexander the Great* (London, 1984) has wonderful illustrations, but might seem to some readers over-confident in its assertions.

A recent technical discussion is N. V. Sekunda, 'The Sarissa', *Acta Universitatis Lodziensis*, 23 (2001), pp. 13–41.

The first attempt at a 'Keegan-style' treatment of Macedonian warriors is A. B. Lloyd, 'Philip II and Alexander the Great: the moulding of Macedon's army', in A. B. Lloyd (ed.), *Battle in Antiquity* (London and Swansea, 1996), pp. 169–98.

Good introductions to light infantry in antiquity are J. G. P. Best, *Thracian Peltasts and Their Influence on Greek Warfare* (Groningen, 1969); and J. K. Anderson, *Military Theory and Practice in the Age of Xenophon* (Berkeley and Los Angeles, 1970), pp. 111–140.

The legionary

The development of the Roman legions can be found in L. Keppie, *The Making of the Roman Army* (London, 1984); and G. Webster, *The Roman Imperial Army* (3rd edn, London, 1985).

Splendid surveys are provided by M. C. Bishop and J. C. N. Coulston, *Roman Military Equipment* (London, 1993); and M. Feugère, *Weapons of the Romans* (English tr., Stroud, 2002).

Among the growing number of 'Keegan-style' analyses are A. K. Goldsworthy, *The Roman Army at War 100 BC to AD 200* (Oxford, 1996); A. D. Lee, 'Morale and the Roman experience of battle', in A. B. Lloyd (ed.), *Battle in Antiquity* (London and Swansea, 1996), pp. 199–217; P. Sabin, 'The face of Roman battle', *Journal of Roman Studies*, 90 (2000), pp. 1–17; A. Zhmodikov, 'Roman Republican heavy infantrymen in battle (IV–II centuries BC)', *Historia*, 49 (2000), pp. 67–78; and G. Daly, *Cannae: The Experience of Battle in the Second Punic War* (London and New York, 2002).

The cavalry

General introductions to mounted warfare are J. Ellis, *Cavalry* (Newton Abbot, 1978); and J. Keegan and R. Holmes, *Soldiers* (London, 1985), pp. 77–96.

Academic studies include G. R. Bugh, *The Horsemen of Athens* (Princeton, 1988); I. G. Spence, *The Cavalry of Classical Greece* (Oxford, 1993); L. J. Worley, *Hippeis: The Cavalry of Ancient Greece* (Boulder, Colorado, and Oxford, 1994); R. E. Gaebel, *Cavalry Operations in the Ancient Greek World* (Norman, 2002); K. R. Dixon and P. Southern, *The Roman Cavalry* (London, 1992); J. B. McCall, *The Cavalry of the Roman Republic* (London and New York, 2002); and I. P. Stephensen and K. R. Dixon, *Roman Cavalry Equipment* (Stroud and Charleston, SC, 2003).

Motivation: only a few fight?

Only 25% fight in S. L. A. Marshall, *Men against Fire* (New York, 1947); 37–55% in S. L. A. Marshall, *Infantry Operations and Weapons Usage in Korea* (London and Washington, 1988, first published 1952), pp. 4–5; 61–2; and 25% in A. K. Goldsworthy, *The Roman Army at War* (Oxford, 1996), pp. 187–8; 219. For criticism of Marshall's figures, see J. Bourke, *An Intimate History of Killing* (London, 1999), pp. 75–6.

Siege warfare

A splendid overview is P. B. Kern, *Ancient Siege Warfare* (Bloomington and Indianapolis, 1999).

Relevant specialized studies include F. E. Winter, *Greek Fortifications* (London, 1971); A. W. Lawrence, *Greek Aims in Fortification* (Oxford, 1979); J. Maloney and B. Hobley (eds), *Roman Urban Defences in the West* (London, 1983); S. Johnson, *Late Roman Fortifications* (London, 1983); and E. W. Marsden, *Greek and Roman Artillery* (2 vols, Oxford, 1969–71).

References for the literary sources named in the text are: Thucydides 2.71–8; 3.20–4; 51–68 (Plataea); Diodorus Siculus 20.82–8; 91–100 (Rhodes); Julius Caesar, *Gallic War* 7.68–89 (Alesia); Josephus, *Jewish War* 5.47–7.20 (Jerusalem); and Ammianus Marcellinus 19.1.1–8.12 (Amida).

On the archaeology of two specific sieges, see M. I. Rostovtzeff, *The Excavations at Dura Europos* (New Haven, 1936), and Y. Yadin, *Masada* (London, 1966). The latter should be read with N. Ben-Yehuda, *Sacrificing Truth: Archaeology and the Myth of Masada* (New York, 2002), which shows how the excavators interpreted what they found to fit both Josephus' ancient narrative and the desires of modern Israel for a heroic past.

Naval warfare

J. S. Morrison, J. F. Coates, and N. B. Rankov, *The Athenian Trireme* (Cambridge, 2000), which is centred on the reconstruction the *Olympias*, provides an accessible introduction to the subject. Despite being outdated in some areas of interpretation, brief and engaging introductions can also be found in *The Greek and Macedonian Art of War* (Berkeley, Los Angeles, and London, 1957), pp. 29–46, and *The Roman Art of War under the Republic* (Cambridge, Mass., 1940), pp. 29–45, both by F. E. Adcock.

Other useful overviews include L. Casson, *The Ancient Mariners* (2nd edn, Princeton, 1991); J. S. Morrison and R. T. Williams, *Greek Oared Ships* (Cambridge, 1968); J. S. Morrison and J. F. Coates, *Greek and Roman Oared Warships* (Oxford, 1996); and J. Rougé, *Ships and Fleets of the Ancient Mediterranean* (English tr., Middletown, Conn., 1981).

G. F. Bass, *A History of Seafaring based on Underwater Archaeology* (London, 1972) offers a well-illustrated and very broad review.

The economics of ancient naval war can be approached via V. Gabrielsen, *Financing the Athenian Fleet* (Baltimore and London, 1994).

Comparative material comes from N. A. B. Rodger, *The Wooden World* (London, 1986).

Winter quarters: exploring a battle and leadership

Julius Caesar's *Commentaries* are translated into many modern languages.

Two studies of how Caesar presents the battle of Atuatuca are K. Welch, 'Caesar and his officers in the Gallic War commentaries' (pp. 85–110; at 93–7) and A. Powell, 'Julius Caesar and the presentation of massacre' (pp. 111–37; at 115–21), both in K. Welch and A. Powell (eds), *Julius Caesar as Artful Reporter: The War Commentaries as Political Instruments* (London and Swansea, 1998).

On the (lack of) archaeological evidence for Atuatuca, see
E. M. Wightman, *Gallia Belgica* (London, 1985), p. 40. On Kalkriese,
P. S. Wells, *The Battle That Stopped Rome: Emperor Augustus,
Arminius, and the Slaughter of the Legions in the Teutoburg Forest*
(New York and London, 2003) is a model of a book written by an
academic for a popular audience.

T. Rice Holmes, *Caesar's Conquest of Gaul* (2nd edn, London, 1911) is
still useful, despite its age, length, and breathtakingly rude rebuttals
of other scholars' views. More recent, concise, and polite is L. Keppie,
The Making of the Roman Army: From Republic to Empire (London,
1984), pp. 80–102.

On Gallic warfare, see A. K. Goldsworthy, *The Roman Army at War
100 BC to AD 200* (Oxford, 1996), pp. 53–60; L. Rawlings, 'Caesar's
portrayal of Gauls as warriors', in K. Welch and A.Powell (eds.), *Julius
Caesar as Artful Reporter* (London, and Swansea, 1998), pp. 171–92;
and (for pictures) P. Connolly, *Greece and Rome at War* (London, 1981),
pp. 113–26.

That regular troops behind fortifications can usually defy vast numbers
of irregulars is one of the many fascinating conclusions of L. H. Keeley,
War Before Civilization: The Myth of the Peaceful Savage (Oxford,
1996). This wide-ranging and inspirational book has yet to make an
impact on academic studies of classical war.

Two thought-provoking studies of classical generalship, which take
rather different lines from those taken here, are E. L. Wheeler, 'The
general as hoplite', in V. D. Hanson (ed.), *Hoplites: The Classical
Greek Battle Experience* (London and New York, 1991), pp. 121–70; and
A. K. Goldsworthy, '"Instinctive genius": The depiction of Caesar the
general', in K. Welch and A. Powell (eds), *Julius Caesar as Artful
Reporter* (London and Swansea, 1998), pp. 193–219.

Two inspiring comparative works are P. Griffith (ed.), *Wellington
Commander: The Iron Duke's Generalship* (Chichester, 1985); and

J. Keegan, *The Mask of Command* (London, 1987). The latter applies one methodology to generalship in a wide range of cultures, while the former approaches one general from a variety of different angles.

Chapter 7

On the Nasamones, see D. J. Mattingly, *Tripolitania* (London, 1995), pp. 28; 33; 72–3; 173–6, who discusses the war-making of ancient North African tribes at pp. 40–1.

For modern works on the Second Punic War, see above, Chapter 1, Romans and Carthaginians.

On the Arab conquests, as on so much else, G. E. M. de Ste. Croix, *The Class Struggle in the Ancient Greek World* (London, 1981), pp. 483–4, offers a brilliantly succinct survey of the underlying issues.

Although it was written a long time ago, has no annotation, and takes the naive line of trying to synthesize (without saying how) the often irreconcilable sources into one narrative, J. B. Glubb, *The Great Arab Conquests* (London, 1963) has the merits of being written by an author who knew intimately the geography of the relevant places, and who had commanded Arab troops there. Thus it remains an enjoyable introduction to the subject.

For scholarly discussions of the Arab conquest of Syria, see, from the Byzantine point of view, W. E. Kaegi, *Byzantium and the Early Islamic Conquests* (Cambridge, 1992); and W. E. Kaegi, *Heraclius Emperor of Byzantium* (Cambridge, 2003), pp. 229–64; and, from the Islamic perspective, F. Gabrieli, *Muhammad and the Conquests of Islam* (English tr., London, 1968), pp. 145–66; and F. M. Donner, *The Early Islamic Conquests* (Princeton, 1981), pp. 91–155.

The military forces of the two sides are set in the context of their historical development by J. Haldon, *Warfare, State and Society in the Byzantine World, 565-1204* (London, 1999); and H. N. Kennedy,

The Armies of the Caliphs: Military and Society in the Early Islamic State (London, 2001).

Three modern reconstructions of the battle of Yarmuk are W. E. Kaegi, *Byzantium and the Early Islamic Conquests* (Cambridge, 1992), pp. 112–46; D. Nicolle, *Yarmuk 636 AD: The Muslim Conquest of Syria* (London, 1994); and J. Haldon, *The Byzantine Wars* (Stroud, 2001), pp. 56–66.

A complete photographic record of the sculptures on the column of Marcus Aurelius can be found in C. Caprino *et al.*, *La Colonna di Marco Aurelio* (Rome, 1955).

A traditional introduction to the column is given by D. E. E. Kleiner, *Roman Sculpture* (New Haven and London, 1992), pp. 295–301.

Among the interesting, if at times heavily theoretical, articles collected in J. Scheid and V. Huet (eds), *Autour de la Colonne Aurélienne* (Turnhout, 2000), those of P. Zanker ('Die Frauen und Kinder der Barbaren auf der Markussäule', pp. 163–74) and J. Balty ('L'Armée de la colonne Aurélienne: images de la cohésion d'un corps', pp. 197–203) are of particular relevance to our concerns here, while that of M. Beard ('The spectator and the column: reading and writing the language of gesture', pp. 265–79) offers a lively introduction to the possibilities and problems of interpreting these, and by extension other, sculptures.

Vegetius is translated, with useful introduction and notes, by N. P. Milner, *Vegetius: Epitome of Military Science* (2nd edn, Liverpool, 1996). For Vegetius in medieval times, see P. Contamine, *War in the Middle Ages* (English tr., Oxford, 1994).

J. A. Lynn, *Battle: A History of Combat and Culture from Ancient Greece to Modern America* (Boulder, Colorado, and Oxford, 2003) provides a good overview of the later influences of classical war in the course of his attack on the reality of the 'Western Way of War' as a continuity of practice.

Chronology

The 'periods' into which modern historians conventionally divide ancient history are in bold, with Roman periods in italics.

1575/50–1100 BC	**Mycenaean Greece**
1200 BC	Trojan War?
1100–776 BC	**Dark-Age Greece**
934–609 BC	Neo-Assyrian empire
776–479 BC	**Archaic Greece**
753–509 BC	*Regal Period at Rome*
c. 750 BC onwards	Emergence of the Greek *polis* (city state)
c. 750–550 BC	Greek 'Age of Colonization'
c. 725–650 BC	Greek invention of hoplite phalanx?
550–330 BC	Achaemenid Persian empire
509–287 BC	*Early Roman Republic*
490–479 BC	Persian Wars
490 BC	Battle of Marathon
480 BC	Battle of Thermopylae
480 BC	Battle of Artemisium
480 BC	Battle of Salamis
479 BC	Battle of Plataea

479–323 BC	**Classical Greece**
472 BC	Aeschylus' *The Persians* first performed
432–430 BC	Athenian siege of Potidaea
431–404 BC	Peloponnesian War
431–427 BC	Spartan siege of Plataea
430 BC	Athenians win naval battle of Naupactus against Spartans
415–413 BC	Athenian expedition to Sicily
405 BC	Athenians lose naval battle of Aegospotami to the Spartans
405–367 BC	Dionysius I, tyrant of Syracuse
371 BC	Thebans beat Spartans at battle of Leuctra
362 BC	Thebans beat Spartans at battle of (Second) Mantinea
359–336 BC	Reign of Philip II of Macedon
338 BC	Philip II defeats a coalition of Greeks at Chaeronea
336–323 BC	Reign of Alexander the Great
333 BC	Alexander defeats the Persians at the battle of Issus
323–30 BC	**Hellenistic Greece**
305–304 BC	Demetrius besieges Rhodes
287–133 BC	***Middle Roman Republic***
264–241 BC	First Punic War
247 BC–AD 224	Parthian (Arsacid) empire
218–201 BC	Second Punic War (Hannibal's War)
214–205 BC	First Macedonian War
213–211 BC	Roman siege of Syracuse
200–196 BC	Second Macedonian War
197 BC	Romans defeat Macedonians at battle of Cynoscephalae
192–189 BC	Roman war with Antiochus III (Selucid king)
171–168 BC	Third Macedonian War
149–147 BC	Macedonian Revolt (Macedon made a Roman province)

146 BC	Greece added to Roman province of Macedonia
149–146 BC	Third Punic War
133–30 BC	***Late Roman Republic***
133 BC	Tiberius Gracchus, a Tribune of the Plebs, enacts land reform
133 BC	Kingdom of Pergamum made Roman province of Asia
107 BC	Marius, a Consul, enrols the unpropertied in the Legions
63 BC	Death of Mithridates VI of Pontus
63–2 BC	Conspiracy of Catiline
58–50 BC	Julius Caesar conquers Gaul
54–53 BC (winter)	Gauls defeat Romans under Sabinus at Atuatuca
53 BC	Parthians defeat Romans at battle of Carrhae, death of Crassus
52 BC	Julius Caesar besieges Alesia
48 BC	Julius Caesar defeats Republicans led by Pompey at Pharsalus
47 BC	Julius Caesar defeats Pharnaces II of Pontus at Zela
46 BC	Julius Caesar defeats Republicans at Thapsus
44 BC	Assassination of Julius Caesar
30 BC–AD 235	***The Principate (Early, or High, Roman empire)***
30 BC–AD 14	Reign of Augustus
AD 9	Germans defeat Romans under Varus in Teutoburg Forest
AD 14–16	Roman campaigns under Germanicus against the Germans
AD c. 40–c. 112	Life of Dio Chrysostom
AD 43	Roman invasion of Britain under Claudius
AD c. 50–c. 120	Life of Plutarch
AD c. 55–c. 135	Life of Epictetus
AD 73/74	Roman siege of Jewish fortress of Masada

AD 83	Romans under Agricola defeat Caledonians at Mons Graupius
AD 86	Domitian's forces defeat the Nasamones
AD 98	Tacitus' *Agricola* written
AD 122–6	Hadrian's Wall built
AD c. 139/42–154/8 and c. 158–64	Occupation of the 'Antonine Wall' in northern Britain
AD c. 160–220	Life of Tertullian
AD 172–5	Marcus Aurelius fights the Germans and Sarmatians
AD 180–92	Reign of Commodus/ construction of Column of Marcus Aurelius
AD c. 185–254	Life of Origen
AD 193–211	Reign of Septimius Severus
AD 224	Sassanid Persians overthrow Parthians

AD 235–84	***The 'Third Century Crisis' of the Roman empire***
AD 235–8	Reign of Maximinus Thrax
AD c. 257	Sassanid Persian siege of Dura-Europos

AD 284–476	***The Dominate (Late, or Low, Roman empire)***
AD 307–37	Reign of Constantine the Great
AD 354–430	Life of Saint Augustine
AD 357	Battle of Strasburg
AD 359	Sassanid Persian siege of Amida
AD c. 370	Huns appear in the Roman world
AD 378	Goths defeat the Romans at the battle of Adrianople
AD 451	'Romans' defeat the Huns at the battle of Chalons
AD 475–6	Reign of last western Roman emperor, Romulus Augustulus

AD 476–1453	***The Byzantine empire***
AD 604–29	Wars between Byzantium and Sassanid Persia
AD 632–3	Ridda (Apostasy) wars in Arabia
AD 633–40	Arabs conquer Syria from Byzantines

AD 636	Arabs defeat Byzantines at battle of Yarmuk
AD 642	Arabs conquer Egypt from Byzantines
AD 651	Fall of the Sassanid Persian Empire
AD 1453	Fall of Constantinople to the Turks
AD 1812/16–28	Rise of Zulu army (reign of Chaka)
AD 1976	John Keegan's *The Face of Battle*
AD 1976	Edward Luttwak's *The Grand Strategy of the Roman Empire*
AD 2000	Ridley Scott's *Gladiator*

Chronology

Index

Visit the
VERY SHORT INTRODUCTIONS
Web site

www.oup.co.uk/vsi

- ➤ **Information** about all published titles

- ➤ News of **forthcoming books**

- ➤ **Extracts** from the books, including titles not yet published

- ➤ **Reviews** and views

- ➤ **Links** to other **web sites** and main OUP web page

- ➤ Information about **VSIs in translation**

- ➤ **Contact** the editors

- ➤ **Order** other **VSIs** on-line

CLASSICS
A Very Short Introduction
Mary Beard and John Henderson

This Very Short Introduction to Classics links a
haunting temple on a lonely mountainside to the glory
of ancient Greece and the grandeur of Rome, and to
Classics within modern culture – from Jefferson and
Byron to Asterix and Ben-Hur.

'The authors show us that Classics is a "modern" and
sexy subject. They succeed brilliantly in this regard …
nobody could fail to be informed and entertained – and
the accent of the book is provocative and stimulating.'

John Godwin, *Times Literary Supplement*

'Statues and slavery, temples and tragedies, museum,
marbles, and mythology – this provocative guide to the
Classics demystifies its varied subject-matter while
seducing the reader with the obvious enthusiasm and
pleasure which mark its writing.'

Edith Hall

HISTORY
A Very Short Introduction
John H. Arnold

History: A Very Short Introduction is a stimulating essay about how we understand the past. The book explores various questions provoked by our understanding of history, and examines how these questions have been answered in the past. Using examples of how historians work, the book shares the sense of excitement at discovering not only the past, but also ourselves.

'A stimulating and provocative introduction to one of collective humanity's most important quests – understanding the past and its relation to the present. A vivid mix of telling examples and clear cut analysis.'

David Lowenthal, University College London

'This is an extremely engaging book, lively, enthusiastic and highly readable, which presents some of the fundamental problems of historical writing in a lucid and accessible manner. As an invitation to the study of history it should be difficult to resist.'

Peter Burke, Emmanuel College, Cambridge

ONLINE CATALOGUE
A Very Short Introduction

Our online catalogue is designed to make it easy to find your ideal Very Short Introduction. View the entire collection by subject area, watch author videos, read sample chapters, and download reading guides.

http://fds.oup.com/www.oup.co.uk/general/vsi/index.html

SOCIAL MEDIA
Very Short Introduction

Join our community
www.oup.com/vsi

- Join us online at the official Very Short Introductions **Facebook** page.
- Access the thoughts and musings of our authors with our online **blog**.
- Sign up for our monthly **e-newsletter** to receive information on all new titles publishing that month.
- Browse the full range of Very Short Introductions online.
- Read **extracts** from the Introductions for free.
- Visit our library of **Reading Guides**. These guides, written by our expert authors will help you to question again, why you think what you think.
- If you are a teacher or lecturer you can order inspection copies quickly and simply via our website.